M

MY STORY

The Autobiography of Olga Korbut

Olga Korbut
with
Ellen Emerson-White

ARROW

Arrow Books Limited
20 Vauxhall Bridge Road, London SW1V 2SA

An imprint of Random House UK Ltd

London Melbourne Sydney Auckland Johannesburg
and agencies throughout the world

Produced by Byron Preiss Visual Publications Inc.

First published by Century, 1992
Arrow Edition, 1993

1 3 5 7 9 10 8 6 4 2

Printed and bound in Great Britain by
Cox & Wyman Ltd, Reading, Berkshire

ISBN 0 09 923131 X

Prologue

The first time I stood on the high balance beam, I felt like a pilot who had climbed up to the stratosphere. Right away, I fell off, hurting my knee. I lay there, on the floor, very close to tears.

Immediately, my coach, Ren, was at my side.

'What's the matter, does it hurt?' he asked impatiently.

Yes. It hurt. I wanted to quit.

'Get up, and let's try it again,' he said. 'Try to be more relaxed. This is not a tightrope, or even the beam. This is a *meadow*. Wherever you put your foot, you will find solid ground. Mount it again.'

I hated him at such moments. After every fall, instead of expressing his concern and pity for this poor, unhappy child, he would just drive me back on to the same terrifying apparatus.

I was too young to know that this was the greatest wisdom that a coach can have. After a fall, a tiny molecule of fear is born, somewhere deep in the soul. If time is lost – even an hour or two – that molecule will grow into an enormous beast. This beast will push you off the apparatus every time you climb on to it, and one day, you will simply be too scared to approach it at all.

After every fall, Ren would make me repeat the same move ten, twenty, or even thirty times, until it was forgotten and that nagging molecule of fear was erased.

So, I got up, hating the beam, hating my coach, and *really* hating that non-existent meadow. I could do a back flip perfectly on a low beam – why was it so important to do it on the high one? None of the other gymnasts ever had to do back flips on the high beam.

The next moment, I was falling again, landing astride the hard wooden beam. The pain was terrific.

'What's the matter?' my coach demanded. 'Are you scared?'

Of course, I was scared. Who wouldn't be?

'See how wide that beam is,' Ren said. 'A real meadow. Right? Let's get started.'

I didn't move.

'Come on, you can't be frightened,' he said. 'The Olympic gold is going to be yours!'

Those last words ruined the entire pep talk. *Me*, an Olympic champion? There was no way that he was going to lure me back on to the beam with a lie like that. He was a chatterbox, and a liar.

'Come *on*,' he urged.

As I hesitated, standing in front of the high, narrow beam, Ren lost his temper.

'You'll never amount to anything,' he said. 'You're a weakling! Even Pirogova' – one of the other girls he coached – 'can work on the beam.' He turned to leave. 'I'm wasting my time here. You're never going to be any good.'

Furious, I climbed back up on to the high beam.

'Don't you say such things to me!' I shouted. 'I'll never amount to anything? Pirogova does the flip better than *I* do?' I was so angry that I did a back flip, perfectly. 'There you are!' I did another. 'There! There! And – one more!'

Ren stood there, with his arms folded, trying to hide his sly grin.

'Okay, good,' he said, and then he smiled. 'Now, do it again.'

Chapter One

For a long time, gymnastics was a taboo word in my home. I had devoted thirteen years to the sport, and too many of my memories were painful. Once I had retired from active competition, I wanted to blot out my past. There was no Munich! No Montréal! No hateful gymnastics with its sweat, its injuries, and its calloused, magnesium-stained palms!

And yet − it wouldn't go away. I wanted to understand myself, and my life, and gymnastics is a very big part of that. I wrote a book called *Once Upon a Time There Lived a Little Girl*, but when it was published in the Soviet Union, it turned out to be little more than an advertisement brochure about an Olympic Champion's life. The not always clean and attractive truth was transformed into a beautiful, and false, fairy tale. Once again, the thick fog of lies which enveloped everyone, and everything, related to top-level Soviet sports had triumphed.

It is only now that I am away from the USSR that I have started to learn the most important rule of life in my Motherland: Do not reach too high. Do not stick your neck out. Those around you, who are not capable of doing what you can do, may not like it. Everyone is supposed to be just like everyone else, like a country full of little broiler chickens. That way, everybody feels fine, and nobody's pride is hurt.

I could never live like that, and I never will.

I also wonder if I will *ever* understand Renald Ivanovich Knysh, my coach. He was the most important person in my life for so long, and I both worshipped, and fought him. I could never accept his philosophy that a gymnast is not an

1

artist in her own right, but just raw material in the hands of a coach.

Our two egos have been battling for nearly twenty years, and I realize now that it is a war that neither of us will ever win. Yet I want to understand him, because if I don't, I will never understand who that little 'wonder girl with pigtails' was, and how she got to be who she is today.

I *need* to understand.

The only thing I know for certain is that I was born to be a gymnast.

I was born in the town of Grodno, in Belorussia (known today as Belarus). My family was very poor, but somehow, when I remember the 180-square-foot room we lived in, I look back to it as a happy, cosy home. Today, I realize that six people – I was the youngest, in a family of four daughters – could not possibly have been comfortable in such a tiny room.

My father, Valentin, worked as a construction engineer, and my mother, Valentina, was a cook in a canteen. They worked from morning until evening, and my sisters and I were on our own. Irina, who is nine years older than I am, was like my second mother. She and Zemfira, my elder by seven years, took good care of Ludmilla and me. Ludmilla is only two years older than I am, but they all thought of me as the baby, and were very protective. Even today, my family don't call me Olga – they call me 'Malaya', which is Belorussian for 'the little one'. It's kind of funny that, after all these years, they still don't quite take me seriously because I'm the baby.

I think my father's life was heavily influenced by his combat experiences in the Second World War – known in Russia as the Great Patriotic War. My father was only fifteen when the fascists came and occupied his village, but he immediately joined the other men from the area in guerrilla activities. He took part in many missions, including blowing up German troop trains and other forms of sabotage.

During one of these forays, he was badly wounded in the arm. His companions were able to get him to a safe hospital,

2

where the doctors decided that his arm would have to be amputated. But, when he was left alone outside the operating room for a minute, my father decided to take a chance and risk infection rather than accept mutilation. He escaped by jumping out of a nearby window. His arm eventually healed on its own, although it has never since been fully functional.

Later, at a hospital near the front lines, he met a talkative young volunteer named Valentina, and fell in love with her. She, of course, was my future mother.

After the war was over and the town of Grodno had been liberated, my father was put in charge of a District Komsomol (Young Communist) committee, although he was only nineteen. He and my mother were married, and over the next ten years, my sisters and I were born.

Father became a member of the City Executive Committee, and was well respected within the government. He used his position to help dozens of other families resist bureaucratic obstruction and acquire bigger apartments, but he kept his own family crammed into a mediocre room. When my mother reproached him for this, he would cut her short, saying simply that other people were in worse situations, and that we could wait a little longer. Because of this, our life was more difficult than necessary, but my father is a humble and conscientious man, and did not want to take advantage of his political connections.

So, we were very poor. Together, my parents only earned eighty roubles a month. Our greatest daily joy was when my mother came home from work. She would leave very early in the morning, and often not return until 11 p.m. or midnight. In the summer, my sisters and I would still be playing on the street at that hour, and I was always delighted if I was the first to see Mom coming around the corner. We would sprint to her, yelling and screaming hello, and help her carry the bag of left-over food from the canteen back to our room for a late supper.

Sometime during my early childhood, my father began drinking. Although he has long since stopped, he has never discussed why he started. I think that, being an intelligent and honest man, he already saw and understood many things about our nation that people only now, in the 1990s, are starting to comprehend. After taking part in the war, and fighting for the promise of a brighter future, it must have been very hard for him to live in a totalitarian state that seemed to care more about repressing people than helping them. Because he could not speak publicly about his doubts without getting into trouble, it may be that the bottle was his only means of taking refuge from his thoughts.

'Dochka,' my mother would say on many nights, using the loving Russian nickname for a little girl, 'will you go and look for your father?'

So I would go to the nearby pub, the room loud and smoky, and filled with the endless buzz of drunken voices. When I found my father, I would tug at his sleeve. 'Dad, let's go home,' I would say. 'Please, Dad.'

Sometimes, he would submissively follow me, but almost as often, I would run home alone. There were other times when he would return very drunk and chase everyone but me out of the house. Then, because he and I were especially close, he would start talking to me. I don't remember anything he said because my main purpose was to quieten him down, put him to bed, and let the others back into the house. I doubt that I have ever loved anybody as much as him in my whole life, but those were difficult times. I wouldn't even mention my father's drinking problem, but I want to tell the whole truth now.

Even so, we also had many good times as a family. Often, we would go off to pick mushrooms together. While my sisters and I were still deciding which way we should go, my father would appear from nowhere, his basket already half-full with little boletus mushrooms. Sometimes, he would take me aside and generously share his booty. I would immediately run to my sisters to show them how many I had 'found'. My mother would usually contribute to her 'Malaya's' basket, too, so I almost always ended up with far more than my share.

We would also go raspberry-picking. We would all scramble into the bushes and hurry to fill the little glass jars

4

so that we would be able to eat as many as we wanted. I enjoyed the outings, but the truth is I hated the work. It was repetitive and monotonous, and I generally got bored within the first ten minutes. Impatience is hardly my best characteristic. Years later, it stood in my way as my coach Ren laboured to make me perfect each new element of my performances, persuading me to repeat them again and again. I found this aspect of my sport – the constant practice and repetition – extremely tedious.

Although as a family we often had a lot of fun, our poverty made life very difficult. Other children would ridicule me for wearing mended hand-me-down clothes from my sisters. I particularly resented those kids who, though well aware of our many hardships, would disdainfully shout orders as if I were some sort of servant.

I think my resulting inferiority complex helped me develop my mule-like stubbornness and perseverance. I acquired a drive to be a leader, and a desire to surprise and shock people, which I still have to this day. I had a constant urge to go out into the street and do something outrageous to cause everyone's mouths to fall open.

'Look, all of you! Did you see *that*?' my mind would shout, as I performed a cartwheel or did a pratfall.

There was a common yard in Lenin Square, where I lived, and where all the children in the neighbourhood gathered to play. Naturally, I was always looking for new challenges and ways to achieve recognition from the rest of the gang. Vit'ka jumped down from the third floor? Great – I would too. Yurka spat fruit seeds eight metres? Terrific – I would reach nine. Pet'ka stood on his head for two hours? I would try for three. I loved competition, and given the chance, I never had any doubt that I would be the winner.

I have thought often about the nature of success, and have come to the conclusion that, to get to the top, you must first be faced with some form of personal challenge. In my case, poverty and hopelessness were both conditions from which I was desperate to escape. I think that the harder something is to achieve, the harder a person will work. Obviously, it would be stupid to demand that anyone who wants to succeed should immediately take a vow of poverty, in order to develop more drive and motivation. But I know that my background had a lot to do with my own success.

Did I hanker, even then, to become a champion? I don't know. I think I just wanted to surprise people. Or, more accurately, to shock them. To be the first to do things. The one everyone else noticed. If that resulted in a championship, then so be it.

Certainly, there is no question that I always wanted to win.

In the boredom of one hot summer afternoon, we came up with a new neighbourhood competition – to put as many plums as possible inside our mouthes. Our team, composed of kids from poor families, lost to the 'fat-and-sweet', which was what we called the kids from well-off families. My opponent's vast mouth had managed to accommodate seven large plums – one more than I, as our team's representative, had been able to stuff in.

Of course, I could not put up with that, and I asked the winner to give me another chance. With a touch of haughtiness, he looked me over and agreed. Everyone on my team roared with delight as I manage to cram seven plums into my mouth. But I was not satisfied with that. I decided to topple the 'fat-and-sweet' boy from his throne, somehow forcing an eighth large plum into my bulging cheeks.

I was the winner, but I also came very close to choking to death. My team-mates poured a bucket of water over me – which didn't help at all – and their attempts to extract even one of the plums from my mouth failed, as my face went from crimson to pale green. Finally, someone suggested that I squeeze my cheeks and, like a burst of machine-gun fire, the plums shot out of me on to the ground, at the feet of the ex-champ.

I guess I was always a tomboy. Being born a girl was the greatest disappointment of my childhood. I think my father had always dreamed of having a son, and maybe some of his dreams were realized in my impish, rambunctious personality. Whenever I asked him, though, he would just grin.

My mother would alter my sisters' old dresses for me, but I couldn't stand wearing them. I didn't care for lace or ribbons, or any of the other things little girls were supposed to enjoy. In fact, I wasn't even sure if I liked little girls, so sedate and demure, chattering incessantly as they played with their stupid dolls. *I* found it much more exciting to climb over a high fence into the fruit garden which belonged to the City Party Executive Committee, and steal some green apples – at the risk of being pelted by a charge of rock salt from the old guard's shotgun.

We climbed over that high fence regularly. We even invented a rather sophisticated device which allowed us to harvest a maximum crop at a minimal risk. We fixed a blade and a sack at the end of a long pole, and if we were skilful enough, we could cut apples right into the sack from the other side of the fence. But this wasn't very thrilling, since there was no risk whatsoever.

As I grew older, I sometimes felt ashamed of our garden raids because it was stealing. But, other than a desire to eat apples, we mainly did it to feel that adrenalin rush of risk. Later we could boast to other friends about our dangerous adventures.

The City Council's fruit garden was the greatest challenge. It was very exciting to climb over the fence, fill the inside of your shirt with apples, and know that somewhere near by there was a guard with a double-barrelled shotgun.

One day, I was sitting in the very top of an apple tree, enjoying my harvest without a care in the world.

Then I heard, 'Get down, Dochka. You might kill yourself.'

I glanced down and saw the old guard standing there, smiling at me. He was pointing his gun, but he didn't seem angry at all.

'I will not,' I said.

'Are you going to sit there all night?' he asked.

I kept eating. 'Yes.'

'Get down. I won't hurt you.'

'If you go away, then I'll get down,' I said, proud of my defiance.

He took several steps back. I scampered down, and started running.

'Hey, Dochka, where are you going?' he called after me. 'What about the apples?'

I looked back, and saw the old man collecting the spilled apples and putting them into my abandoned sack.

'Here,' he said. 'Take them. And come again, I'll give you more!'

I didn't ever return to the City Council garden. What was the point? There was no thrill left, no danger. The 'risk' had been a figment of our imaginations. Besides, in all honesty, I would have been ashamed to see that old man again.

In search of a more interesting and breathtaking escapade, we turned to the orchards of private owners, knowing that they certainly would not give away any apples. And, at first, everything was fine. Several raids produced ample loot and some excitement. But then, we got more of a thrill than we had bargained for.

It was a nice day, and I led my team to a splendid orchard. A little boy from a neighbouring yard had threatened that if he couldn't come, he would tell on us, so we had been forced to let him join us. We used him for a look-out, and then approached the house. We watched it for a while, decided nobody was home, and embarked on our raid. We were going about our business in the well-tended orchard when, unobserved, a man came out on to the porch of the house.

The first to see him was the little boy who had come along at the last minute. He panicked, and started to run. The man dashed after him, giving the rest of us an opportunity to escape.

Reaching the security of our yard in Lenin Square, we chattered about our splendid experience, none of us even considering the possibility that the owner might have managed to catch his victim. In fact, he had, and the boy gave him all our names and addresses.

I didn't find out about this until a week later, when the prank was nearly forgotten. Then, suddenly, a militia officer appeared at our door.

'Are you Olga Korbut?' he asked sternly.

I nodded.

'Report to the militia station by 4 p.m.' He turned and left without a smile.

I was both frightened and excited by this prospect. But when I got to the station, my mother's best friend, Katya, was waiting for me. She was our district militia officer.

She looked at me for a minute. 'Well, Olga, did you enjoy the fruit you pinched?' she asked finally.

As reprimands went, that was pretty mild, but my friends and I decided to reduce the risk from then on, and use our pole, blade and sack device exclusively. It was dull, but it was safe.

I was still very young, but my personality was by now almost completely formed. I had always been stubborn and irreverent, rebelling fiercely against common norms and rules of behaviour. Obviously, I needed some sort of outlet – other than pranks – for all that energy. I yearned to prove to everyone that I was an individual with a right to self-expression. Of course, this was not a typical attitude for a little girl in the Soviet Union to have, and people always described me as 'salt an'd pepper'. Emphasis on the pepper, I think.

Little did I know that I was about to discover something that would change my life. Or, maybe, gymnastics discovered *me* first. Perhaps everyone gets to choose an individual road, but I think that my road had come looking for me.

Either way, my carefree childhood was about to come to a premature end.

Chapter Two

My gymastics career began on that October morning in the second grade when, during our Russian language lesson, the door opened and Yaroslav Ivanovich Korol, our physical culture instructor, walked in.

After apologizing for the interruption, he said, 'We are setting up a gymnastic section here at the school. The exercises are going to be twice a week. Is there anyone who wants to join?'

Before that, I had only attended physical culture lessons twice a week, and now I would have four of them. How could I miss such a chance? So, I raised my hand.

It was my first step along the road.

A dozen or so second-graders came to the first session, but we didn't get to do anything. Yaroslav Korol spoke for a long time about how beautiful the world of gymnastics was, and what discoveries and wonders awaited those who were looking for them. His colourful and passionate speech had very little effect on me. I was not interested in hearing about unattainable heights. All I wanted to do was to start practising.

Then, Korol asked one girl, who was several years older and studied at a sports school, to show us some exercises. She walked elegantly about the gym, waving her arms and extending her pointed leg just like a real ballerina. To us, all untrained, awkward kids, she was like a magical pixie. To conclude her performance, she did a vault, and some splits and rolls – all so lightly and so effortlessly!

As I watched her spin and jump and dance, my self-confidence faded. Would I ever be as lithe and graceful? My normal urge always to come first, to be centre stage, was failing me. Not only did she seem more talented than I was, but I was still feeling the effects of a recent, rather embarrassing experience.

Like any child, I loved going to the circus. I would step inside the big top and lapse into a state of euphoria, only recovering my senses when the master of ceremonies announced, 'The show is over!'

I had seen a circus performer walking on a tightrope while rotating a container of water in a full circle on his open palm. Not a single drop of water spilled and, not understanding the physics of centrifugal force, I couldn't figure out how he had managed such a miraculous feat.

I decided to explore this puzzle under very inappropriate circumstances. Every morning, my mother gave me twenty-four kopecks and an empty flask, so that I could buy a litre of milk at the nearest store. I would wait in the endless queue, my muscles bursting with the impatient energy of youth. Finally, I would buy the milk, and start walking briskly home, drinking from the flask as I went. Not wanting to get caught, I would replenish the missing milk with tap water before I got home. Then, adding to this diluted mixture, my mother would pour yet another litre of water into the breakfast porridge. Only I knew how little milk there really *was* in the blend.

One morning, as I was returning from the store, I thought about the tightrope walker and his amazing feat with the container of water. But I didn't want to experiment in view of my mother, so, after pouring the daily mix of water and milk into a pan, I refilled the flask with plain water and went outside. Grasping the flask by the handle, I started to imitate the circus performer. As I spun it over my head, the water gushed out all over me. Every single drop.

I continued practising, and learned the importance of speed in spinning the flask. Even though for a second the flask was upside down, the contents didn't spill if my arm moved fast enough.

The next day, as soon as I had left the store and drunk my share of undiluted milk, I practised my act again. This time, though, the milk was still in the flask. My timing was fine, but the quality of the packaging let me down. Before the final part of my gravity-defying act, the handle of the flask broke away, and by the time it hit the ground, it was empty.

I was terrified. For the first time in my life, my family was not going to be able to have its traditional porridge for breakfast, and it was all my fault. I hid in the bushes all day long, trying to invent a more or less truthful excuse for my accident. I thought of a hundred stories – a miraculous escape from the local train, a courageous rescue of a child, and so on – but to no avail.

When it started to get dark, I knew I had to go home. I crawled stealthily into my yard, wondering how severe my punishment was going to be. The first person I saw was my sister Ludmilla, and after exchanging the necessary information, she agreed to carry the flag of truce to my parents.

Fortunately, the negotiations were successful.

'Come home,' Ludmilla said, returning to me. 'Everything's fine.'

By now, I was more ashamed than scared, and I slowly approached the house with my head bowed.

'Dochka, we've been looking all over Grodno for you!' my mother shouted from the balcony.

'Mommy, I spilled the milk,' I wailed.

I imagine the quantity of tears shed that day just about equalled the amount of spilled milk.

Recalling that incident, still vivid in my memory, I mentally compared my abilities to the skilled gymnast from the sports school, and I felt very dismal.

Seeing the worried expressions on our faces, Korol laughed. 'You dragonflies will be able to do the same things soon,' he promised. 'Now, everybody up, on the double, one, two, three. . . .'

After that, the momentum of life increased, although there were many times when it seemed to crawl instead of fly. At each gymnastics session, I put in as much energy as I had spent climbing fences and stealing apples; yet I felt we were wasting time, and needed to focus more on the basics. We only visited the gym twice a week, and it just wasn't enough. I learned push-ups and pikes, walking on a bench, and stretches – all the gymnastics ABCs. Almost from the very beginning, however, my muscles required new challenges.

I don't want to offend Ren Knysh, but Yaroslav Ivanovich Korol was truly the first person to discover me. He quickly realized that all the exercises were very easy for me, and that I needed more to do. So he would give me extra, more complicated assignments than he gave the other girls. I mastered all of them easily and felt, for the first time in my life, that I was committed to something of value.

I would feel especially proud when the other girls had trouble performing an exercise and Korol would turn to me and say, 'Olga, will you demonstrate to the folks?'

I took immense pleasure in showing off, finding it *much* more rewarding than shoving an eighth plum into my cheek.

Then came a moment which, although expected, nevertheless came as a complete surprise.

'There is going to be a Grodno City Gymnastics Meet for school children and we are entering for it,' Korol told us. 'Remember, the best will be selected for the Red Banner Sports School, so get ready.'

There was no question that I was prepared, but my family's poverty became an issue. At school, we exercised in tights and half-shoes that we called 'Czech shoes', but now we would need leotards and special white gymnastics shoes. Where would I be able to get them? And how could I justify asking my family for such an expense, even for the first important championship meet of my life? After all, there were six mouths to feed.

My mother took care of everything. She made a leotard out of a long T-shirt and a safety pin, and cobbled a pair of shoes from a white towel. If you had a vivid imagination, they looked exactly like white gymnastics shoes. Necessity makes people quite resourceful!

On the day of the meet, I awoke before the sun rose. The competition was scheduled for 3 p.m, in the gym at the Red Banner Stadium – hours away, but I didn't think I could wait that long. I felt a strange mixture of anxiety, happiness and dread, and I paced around the room, managing to wake up my entire family in the process. At first, they were angry, but then they understood and tried to calm me down.

By noon, I was already at the gym. There wasn't a single empty seat anywhere in the stands, and I stood in the crowd, looking down at the gym floor. All I could see were 'the fat and sweet' – well-groomed, self-confident girls in perfect, brightly coloured leotards. And there I was, with that damned safety pin.

The judges called on the girls one at a time. They would bow coquettishly and start to perform their routines. Most of them were very good, doing tricks we had never even heard of, and I began to make comparisons, trying to guess our school's odds. On the whole, our chances were pretty good, I felt, as long as my terry-cloth galoshes and the safety pin held together.

While our own routines were simple, they were no worse than the others. For example, an ordinary exercise on the uneven parallel bars could be very rich in content. You would mount the low bar, by any method, sit on it for several seconds, trying not to rock, wave both hands simultaneously at the audience and then return to the initial position as gracefully as possible.

We were so small that we couldn't climb up on the balance beam without some help, so the judges would allow us to use a chair. After you managed to get on the beam, all you had to do was walk its length twice, and then jump down. The most important thing was to spread your arms elegantly upon landing. My team-mates and I were very good at the floor exercises, which were actually traditional 'Kaleenka' dances, with a few gymnastic moves added.

'No problem,' I decided, watching the other girls perform. 'We can do this.'

My team-mates arrived dead on time, and when they saw our well-schooled competitors, they panicked.

'Girls, I've been here three hours,' I said confidently. 'I've seen everything. Nothing to be afraid of – we'll show them what it's all about.'

15

Korol smiled at my bragging, but echoed me in promising that we would certainly 'show them'.

It may be hard to believe, but I can't remember that first official performance of mine at all. The only recollection I have is worrying that my safety pin might open at the wrong moment.

After a long wait for the judges' decisions, we found out that our team had placed among the top three, but that individually, none of us had made it into the top ten. Once the results had been posted, we all lined up and the sports school coaches started picking those who, in their opinions, should receive serious training.

I soon realized that I didn't stand a chance. The coaches were only choosing skinny girls. None of them were interested in my strongly built figure; and all the starved-looking girls they snatched from either side of me just happened to be sporting great big bows in their hair and wearing bright, cheerful leotards.

'Weight?' the coaches would ask. 'Height? Date of birth? All right, please come to such and such a place at such and such a time. . . .'

It was humiliating. They selected girls the way ranchers choose livestock at a horse auction: examining teeth, tapping at joints, and paying particular attention to the groin area. Most importantly, though, none of them was paying the slightest attention to *me*.

Then I had a stroke of luck. Elena Volchetskaya herself, a former Olympic champion – the idol of us all – came up to me and spoke the words I had only dreamed of hearing.

'Well, "fatty",' she said. 'Want to go to a sports school?'

Talk about stupid questions.

Today, when I recall that process of selection, I can't find a good explanation for it. Who decided girls should be chosen because of their builds? Fat or thin, what difference does it make? You can always lose extra pounds or, if necessary, put on weight. What an athlete needs most is a strong character, and the will to succeed. Is that only found in thin people?

Years later, when I became a coach myself, I vowed never to use a girl's build as a criterion for selecting her. I have always preferred to get to know each of them, and then watch them at practice sessions. Decisions on that basis will be fair. It is much less degrading, and you won't overlook a strong-willed 'fatty'.

Why did Elena Volchetskaya choose me? I don't know, since I did not, at that time, meet a single requirement for a gymnast. She herself told me later that I had not looked like much of a prospect to her, so maybe she just felt sorry for me. Then, after she started teaching me, she was very surprised by how well I did.

My main memory of that first year at the sports school is that my life was one long holiday. I have never experienced such a continuously wonderful feeling, before or since. At last, I had a chance to expend all my energy. We practised every day, and I loved it. Volchetskaya had no high hopes for me, but when she saw that 'fatty' didn't shirk any of the menial tasks, she started giving me home assignments.

I enjoyed the homework, but it inflicted some suffering on my family as I turned our little room into a gymnasium. My sisters would sit on the sofa and amuse themselves with rude comments as they watched my stretching, push-ups, kicks, knee-lifts, and the rest. Before I discovered gymnastics, I would have used my fists in response to their sarcasm, but now I ignored them. Something important had come into my life, screening me from the rest of the world.

After my sisters realized that their remarks were having no effect, they stopped bothering me. Clearly they got accustomed to the fact that, every day at the same time, their baby sister would again engage in 'her stupid things'.

My mother was much more understanding about the situation. She probably thought, 'Let this dynamo spend her zillion watts of energy on something useful, rather than on escapades which end in her coming back with her clothes all torn.'

I used to bring a couple of blankets to our ravine, and put on shows for the neighbourhood children. One of the blankets, hung on two poles driven into the ground, served as a curtain, and I used the other for a mat.

I was the orchestra that played stirring march music, and I was also the announcer. The show consisted of simple moves, jumps, and various types of turns and rotations. On my improvised stage, I performed every trick I had been taught, as well as a few of my own. I was so absorbed in my performance that it was only after I bowed at the end that I learned the reason for the absence of applause – my ungrateful audience had left.

In all honesty, the shows were pretty bad, but that ravine was the site of the first performances, private or public, starring the youngest Korbut girl.

The work at the gym progressed at full swing. I was too young to think about what might happen next, and had no idea that only some of us would be allowed to move on to the advanced group. The rest would be labelled 'unpromising', and forgotten.

Nor did I know that Renald Ivanovich Knysh himself, who supervised all the coaches, saw absolutely no reason to keep me in the school. Ren was strongly against the idea of Volchetskaya wasting her time on me. His reasoning was simple: there was no way to make a gymnast out of this 'fatty'.

After he had watched us working for some time, he approached Volchetskaya. 'I can't understand it, Lenka,' he said sternly, but using her nickname. 'Why do you keep her? Don't you have better things to do? Why do you need this dumpling?'

'First of all, this "small ball" works like a mule,' Volchetskaya said with controlled anger. 'And second, she immediately carries out anything you show her. I won't expel her.'

The outcome of this ongoing dispute would determine my whole future. I came very close to being expelled from the school, and it is ironic that the person who argued most strongly in favour of it was to become my coach.

The story that Renald Knysh discovered, selected and trained me is a complete fantasy, created by journalists versed in stereotypes and clichés. Many of them wrote about the mysterious system he used to seek out and select young gymnasts, which helped him to discover Olga Korbut. The only problem with this story is that it never happened.

The reality is much more intriguing. Before he finally accepted me for his group, Ren tried to throw me out of the school on several occasions. He would give Volchetskaya ultimatums, saying things like, 'If this "fatty" doesn't execute a split tomorrow, I won't see her here again.'

Knowing her boss's difficult personality, Volchetskaya would then spend hours explaining and demonstrating the new skills to me. 'Please, Olen'ka, you have to do it,' she would say. 'It is very important.'

So I would go home and spend all my free time working and stretching, providing great fun for my sisters. I didn't know that this was a backbreaking assignment from the great Knysh himself, and my ignorance was probably my good fortune. The next day, I would go in and demurely execute a split, or whatever new skill he demanded. Volchetskaya would smile proudly, and Ren would frown in surprise and confusion.

Paradoxically, I was the only one of Elena Volchetskaya's students that year – the one Knysh disliked so much – who stayed in gymnastics. All the other diligent girls in the group disappeared from the sport without a trace.

Every girl in the school desperately wanted to be transferred into Ren's group. Among his former students were the famous Tamara Alexayeva, who eventually became a coach, and Elena Volchetskaya herself, an Olympic champion. We all thought of Ren's group as a step to the gymnastics Olympus, where you could be crowned with a golden halo.

I have no idea what made Ren change his mind and take me on. Maybe he just started watching me more closely, and decided that with my help, he could challenge the prevailing concepts of gymnastics development. Tall gymnasts were 'in' at that time and I, in addition to being a 'small ball', was also very short. Who knows?

Anyway, one day, Knysh came over to me, and said, 'Well, "fatty", why don't we try a half-turn on this horse?'

I ran straight to the apparatus, even though an element such as the half-turn can only be done by gymnasts who have trained for a long time. Ren gave me a two-hour lecture on the move, how it had to be executed, what difficulties it entailed, and ways to overcome them. I tried to listen, but my thoughts were already up on the horse.

Sensing my impatience, Ren suddenly smiled – a rare occurrence, indeed. A grin from Ren is as rare as a rose in December.

We worked on the vault for two hours. When I did everything he asked, without many faults or problems, he fell into deep thought, and murmured something that made no sense to me.

'Modelling clay,' he said to himself. 'Grasping so fast. . .'

I think he was both surprised and happy, and shocked, by what he was seeing. Just a month earlier, he had told Volchetskaya to get rid of that unpromising 'small ball', who had now, in a mere couple of hours, mastered a vault that would normally require a full six months of training.

I stood in front of him, my eyes wide and eager. 'Anything else, sir?'

He didn't answer right away, but then he sighed.

'Come back tomorrow morning,' he said. 'You're going to join my group.'

Chapter Three

Those few words had the effect of glorious fireworks exploding in my soul. For the next several weeks, I lived in a state of complete bliss, betrayed by occasional incoherent utterances and seemingly unmotivated smiles.

Compared to me, the girls in Ren's group were fairly mature. They had already performed in several meets, and some of them had even earned medals. I immediately considered myself one of them, a member of the élite, and paid no attention to their grumbling. They thought I was inferior to them, an ugly duckling in the company of noble swans. Fortunately, because of my sisters' regular teasing, I had developed an ability to ignore such trifles.

I worked very hard, but for some reason, Ren seemed to have forgotten my existence. In less than a year at the school, in addition to the vault move, I had learned to do a straight split, cartwheels on a wide beam, bridges, and many other moves. I was starving for more challenges but Ren would only allow me to attend one practice in the morning, no matter how often I begged to come to the afternoon session, too.

This may have been because he was still hedging his bets with me, but probably he wanted me to study the basics of gymnastics slowly, giving my body time to get a bit stronger. He was also smart enough not to give me so much work that I would lose my appetite for the sport. Still, I found the unhurried pace very frustrating.

One day, I did a very defiant thing. Even though Ren had said his usual 'See you tomorrow morning', at the end of practice, I gathered up all my nerve and returned to the gym that afternoon.

'Why did you come?' Ren asked, his face expressionless.

I was speechless, unable to tell if he were angry or pleased.

He waited for a minute, and then said, 'Well, okay. Since you're here, start warming up.'

Another year passed. I have two memories of my second year in the sports school: the pain of tired muscles, now that I was attending both daily practices, and the stronger pain of hurt feelings, since Ren never gave me a single kind word. I, who could not live through a day without other people's attention, was forced to accept neglect. What did I have to do – put nine plums in my mouth? I found myself devising ways to get Ren to focus on me.

Easily and faultlessly, I executed all the elements regularly carried out by the older girls. Still, no reaction from Ren. No matter what I did, he ignored me.

One day, however, I finally succeeded. I forget the details but evidently I committed some outrageous misdeed, and *boy*, did I get his attention.

'Get the hell out of here!' Ren screamed at me. 'I won't have you back in this gym, ever!'

So, that was it. Everything was over for me. During the next month, I was miserable. I realized that I couldn't live without gymnastics. The pep talk I gave myself (Screw them all! I'll be fine without them!) was of no help.

A few days later, when it was dark, I went to the gym and peeped through the window to see what they were doing. Everyone looked perfectly normal, as though they hadn't even noticed that I was gone.

I saw Svetlana Semyonovna, the school accompanist, hurrying towards the door, and stopped her.

'How are they doing?' I asked, trying to conceal my desperation. 'How's Ren?'

'Fine,' she said, vaguely, and went inside.

After a month of torture, I couldn't stand it any more. Apprehensively, I went to the gym and knocked on the door – a futile exercise, since there was little chance of anyone hearing me. I took a deep breath, and went inside.

I knew the words I should say: 'Forgive me, please, I won't do it again.' But my tongue felt like cement.

Ren glanced over casually, as though I had never left.

'As usual, tomorrow at six,' he said, and went back to what he was doing.

I know Ren as well as anyone in the world, but I still don't understand him. He is a very strange person: withdrawn and close-mouthed, tough and unpredictable. He could certainly feel emotions – pleasure, irritation, anger – but kept everything hidden deep inside. He didn't cheer or praise; at best, he just acknowledged.

I think that kicking me out of the programme was not just a punishment, but also a cruel test. If I came back, everything was fine and he would go on working with me. If I didn't, it was no great loss because a person that easy to break had no place in the sport.

Yet that was not all. Soon, there was another test in store for me, one that threatened to nip my gymnastics career in the bud.

I was doing an easy balance-beam element when I unexpectedly fell. Trying to cushion my fall, I put out my hand, and felt a searing pain. (Why, I wonder, don't they teach gymnasts how to fall safely, just as they do young judo athletes the very first time they come to the gym?)

I was rushed to the hospital with a fracture of a small bone and a dislocation. The doctors took care of the dislocation at once and put my arm in a cast, but after four weeks, the bone still hadn't shown any signs of healing.

At first, Ren came to visit me in the hospital to see how I was doing, but then he disappeared. I found out that meanwhile he had started training my sister, Ludmilla. The fear of losing Ren made me follow my surgeon like a shadow, nagging him to operate on me as soon as possible. In the meantime, I did my best to stay in shape, building my leg muscles by doing squats and other exercises.

'Aren't you scared?' the surgeon kept asking me. 'It's going to be very painful.'

'No, I'm not,' I lied. He didn't seem to understand that the sooner he did the wretched operation, the sooner I could get back to the gym.

They operated with a local anaesthetic, and the incredible pain I felt when they fastened the cartilage to the bone with metal pins is still fresh in my memory.

My arm was then placed in another cast, but the doctor failed to warn me about how important it was to exercise the arm after the operation. As a result of his negligence, my arm was bent and lifeless when the cast was removed. It looked as though gymnastics really was over for me – permanently. I was devastated.

Once I had been checked out of the hospital, I went to a clinic every day where the physiotherapy specialists tried to revive my arm. But none of the exercises helped. My arm still wouldn't work.

I started training myself to perform all the elements that did not require the use of my injured limb, but I realized I would be unable to go far in gymnastics with such a handicap. No matter how hard I struggled, my arm was frozen in one position.

Suddenly, I found a way out. I sewed some small bags and filled them with sand. When I went to bed at night, I put them on my bad arm. Under the heavy weight, the arm would straighten a bit by the next morning, but bending it was still real torture. I loved gymnastics too much simply to quit. It was hard to force myself to keep trying, but I refused to give up.

Each day at home, I would hear about the great progress Ludmilla was making at the gym. I wasn't exactly jealous, but I was hurt that Ren had dropped me from his life and put someone else in my place.

On the day that I was finally able to return to the gym, Ren was very surprised. I had come back not just to say hello, but to resume working – thanks, after an agonizing struggle, to a completely healthy, agile and obedient arm. The arm had a long, wide row of stitches, so it didn't look very pretty, but it worked.

Some years later, after my triumph in Munich, I ran into the surgeon who had done the operation. He was unable to look me in the eye.

'If I'd known you were to become an Olympic champion, I would have made a very neat little row of stitches,' he muttered. *Now* he tells me. There was no mention of his responsibility for my tortuous recovery.

At the time, however, the most important thing was that I was able to resume my work at the gym after my lengthy forced vacation. Eager to continue learning, I blithely forgave Ren for his lack of support and faith in my ability to return.

Our work went on as usual. Then our class hit a major obstacle. The whole group was trying to learn how to do a backward somersault on the balance beam, but three months of trying had produced nothing but bewilderment and frustration. The feat seemed impossible. Previously, I had been convinced that I could do *anything* if I worked long enough. Now, I had my doubts.

One morning, before Ren arrived, I tried the somersault yet again – and pulled it off. I have no idea how I managed it, but I did a perfect somersault in front of the whole group.

Ren came in and before he could take off his raincoat, the girls had surrounded him.

'Renald Ivanovich!' they shouted. 'Olga did the somersault!'

I stood next to the beam, very proud of myself, waiting for Ren's praise. After all, I'd earned it.

'So what?' he said, which was like a bucket of ice cold water being dumped over my head. 'Why such a din? Will you all be so kind as to start warming up?'

Watching him hang his coat neatly on a hanger, I hated him. This wasn't just another standard element, performed by thousands. I had just done a *back flip* on the beam, the very same feat that would astonish audiences when they saw it performed several years later. It was my first 'ultra C' element, never seen before at an official meet, and my own coach didn't seem impressed.

Looking back, I think I understand why he was silent. Every night, his creative mind fantasized dozens of new gymnastic elements and combinations. The fact that he could not realize all his fantasies was probably his greatest personal tragedy. No matter how hard he tried, he could not implement all the ideas born in his imagination. That is probably why he could not fully appreciate my actual back flip. For him, it was already something he had mentally buried in the past.

In many ways, thinking about Ren makes me sadder than anything else.

'Sure,' his reasoning seemed to be, 'the girl has potential; she's pliant, receptive, supple. Whether she's stupid or too young, she lacks fear, seems not to sense risk or danger. But that sturdy figure of hers ruins her chances. As she gets older, she'll get fatter, and goodbye, gymnastics!'

Yet from then on, he watched me very closely, as if he were waiting. But for what? Until I lost those extra pounds? Until I managed to implement even more of his fantastic notions? Over and over, I would beg him in my mind to notice me. 'Please, look at me, you block of wood!' I would shout inside my head. 'I'm doing my best, you chunk of ice! Tell me how good I am!'

I suspect he finally made up his mind in my favour after the 1966 Liepaya All-Union Meet in Liepaya, Latvia – my first official competition.

At Liepaya, I won my first all-around victory for my age group. I even earned a 10.0 for my routine on the uneven bars. During that meet, I also performed my back flip on the beam for the first time in public. As usual, I got no praise from Ren, but the audience and gymnastics specialists were very enthusiastic. In fact, in the middle of the meet, an Organizing Committee representative asked me to demonstrate several of the elements from my programme, including the back flip.

Naturally, I had no objection to this.

'Ladies and gentleman,' the announcer said with a soft Baltic accent. 'We apologize for the interruption of the competition. We hope you will enjoy having another chance to watch the unusual elements performed by Olga Korbut, the gymnast from Grodno.'

I did the flip a dozen times, drinking in the applause. Later, I was also allowed to take part in the demonstration performances with the very top gymnasts.

This successful reception soothed more than my parched ego. Ren's colleagues enthusiastically surrounded him, bombarding him with questions and compliments. To my amazement, my coach got very flustered and blushed. This was hardly the silent, stolid man I had come to know.

After Liepaya, we started practising six hours a day, until I was completely worn out. But I welcomed the chance to make some real progress.

I remember Liepaya for two more reasons. First of all, I unexpectedly jumped from the modest Third Junior Category straight to the title of Candidate for Master of Sports in Gymnastics. I was progressing even faster than *I* had expected.

I also recall my father running up to the train just seconds before we departed for Latvia. He kissed me, wished me good luck, and inconspicuously put a piece of crumpled paper into my hand.

'Just in case you need it, daughter,' he said.

Inside the car, I opened my fist and discovered that the piece of paper was a five-rouble bill. Five roubles was a great deal of money to my family. Shocked, I closed my fist and decided to save every bit of the money. I figured that when I got home, my parents would be happy that I had been so thoughtful and thrifty. But I went even further, exchanging for cash the food and refreshment coupons our coaches had given us.

When I returned home, I looked proudly at my parents and sisters, and dropped the five-rouble bill and a heap of change on to the table.

There was a moment of total silence, and then my mother went to the kitchen. I could hear her weeping, and I was very confused. Why weren't they pleased?

My father swallowed visibly, and then picked up the money, sticking it back into my pocket.

'Never do that again,' he said quietly. 'Okay, Dochka?'

'Okay,' I replied, still not sure what I had done wrong. I did not realize that my frugality had nullified my parents' gesture of love and pride. But, once I did understand, it was a lesson about respect that I never forgot.

Shortly after the Liepaya meet, I was given a sixty-rouble scholarship. There was no limit to my pride when I brought home my first earnings. This time, my parents shared that pride with me.

By now, Ren and I were working to the limits of our respective abilities. In a sense, he managed to exploit my obstinacy to achieve his goals. Working with him was both pleasant and painful. Sometimes he introduced me gently to risky new elements, but almost as often, he was reckless and cruel. I often felt that he didn't think of me as a human being with bones and muscles and feelings, but as an inanimate piece of clay that he could use to form anything he wanted.

Once, he was sitting on the beam, talking to some of the other coaches, when he suddenly looked up.

'Olga, do a double flip without matting,' he said.

I stared at him, stunned. Nobody had ever performed such a trick before, not even in the circus. But, using a mat, I *had* done it a few times.

'No, Renald Ivanovich,' I said nervously. 'Let me first do it on the mat.'

He took a chocolate bar out of his pocket. 'Want it?' he asked. 'Do the flip.'

His bribery made me angry and I went to the mat and did the double flip. Then, I walked back.

'Give me that candy now,' I demanded.

He offered me a caramel, and I pushed his hand aside.

'You *showed* me a chocolate bar,' I said, enraged by his duplicity.

He shrugged. 'The condition was, no matting.'

I yanked the mat away in an absolute fury, did the flip on the bare floorboards, and he gave me the candy bar. I held his eyes with mine, and then tossed the candy disdainfully away.

If anything, he was amused.

*

After that incident, I never completely trusted him again. He should never have made me risk that double flip (which was still a new element for me) without the mat. What was he trying to prove? Was it so important that he had to risk my life?

'I'll be damned, Ren,' people would say. 'Only a student of yours would do something like that. What part of your body do you use for brains? What if she falls?'

'No big deal,' he would answer. 'She'll get up.'

I was really beginning to resent being thought of as a machine. But, morning after morning, Ren would come to me with a new element, and demand its immediate execution. He would describe to me in great detail what he wanted, down to the very last nuance, and I would try to perform the impossible for him.

'This should be no problem for you,' he would say cheerfully.

But, almost every time, I was terrified by his ambitious notions. He nearly had to drag me over to the uneven bars to work on what was later christened the 'Korbut Loop'. Although the bars later became my favourite apparatus, I hated them at that point in my life because I was too short and could not reach easily from the low bar to the high. This, incidentally, prevented me from receiving the title 'Master of Sports' the first time I was nominated.

Ren wanted to achieve everything at once, but he tried to take things slowly. My growing distrust made me approach each new innovation very carefully.

For example, he installed some special uneven bars with adjustable height. He would pile up mats to ensure a 'soft landing', in case I fell during the back-first flights from bar to bar. The bars started low, and then got higher. At first, the pile of mats also grew higher, and the process continued until the bars stood at their appropriate height and the mats disappeared. That would mean that I had mastered the skill or, at the very least, mastered my fear.

No matter what we did during the two daily practices, at the end Ren would say, 'Now, perform the loop flawlessly, twenty times.'

Twenty times, flawlessly. That meant at least eighty or ninety attempts, after which I would feel elated, already imagining myself in a hot shower, soothing my tired muscles.

But nearly always, Ren would just wince as though he had the world's worst toothache.

'Today, you didn't do it precisely enough,' he would say. 'Try again.'

What did he want? Did he *really* expect to achieve absolute perfection? Determined not to go back to the bars, even under threat of execution, I would sit down on a mat and refuse to move. He would try pleas, logic and threats, none of which worked.

'Okay,' he would say finally. 'Think it over, Olga.'

Then I would hear a click as the door locked behind him. Once I was alone, I felt a little better. After some more private grumbling, I would approach the bars. Suppressing my fatigue, I would force myself to do one more loop, and then another, and so on.

My exercises would be interrupted by the click of the lock.

'At last,' Ren would say, coming back in. 'You just can't live without putting on a show, can you?'

No one but a coach and his pupil can understand the amount of hard work it takes to create a new element. After five years (in retrospect, I am appalled by the time invested!) of working every day, 'twenty times, flawlessly', Ren and I had perfected the 'Korbut Loop'.

Ren, always eager to try new things, hated looking back and realizing that we had spent *five years* on *one* element. I sympathized with him when people started imitating 'my' loop. Suddenly, everyone was doing it. After all our work, it didn't seem quite fair.

At some point during its development, I learned that the loop wasn't just a group of moves that I had to do while not falling. I learned how to subjugate it, how to control it. I knew how to do it, and the move was mine!

The fraction of a second needed to execute it was like an eternity, and I would see myself from somewhere outside my body, as if I were in slow motion. It was easy to correct errors and polish flaws.

Even so, I was always intimidated by the loop. The fear never really disappeared. Every time I approached the bars, I felt icy inside. My cowardly inner voice would whisper, 'Step back, don't do it. You're afraid.' But then I would hear Ren's harsh, 'Now, twenty more times, flawlessly!'

The little coward inside would vanish at the last moment, and I would mount the apparatus with complete confidence.

When I get right down to it, I think I was more frightened by the mental threat of my coach than by the physical fear of falling.

Chapter Four

Many of the meets for which I entered during the following months blur together in my mind. I do remember, though, that a month before the 1967 Belorussian National Championship, a television crew came to Grodno. They had got hold of some information about Renald Knysh's 'secret weapon'. Ren, who hated publicity, was able to outwit the journalists, and instead of an 'Olga Korbut – Secret Weapon' programme, the crew had to be content with a more mundane 'Problems of Gymnastic Education Methods'.

The cameraman filmed my loop routine, and I was excited by the prospect of being a television star, but Ren refused to allow them to use the material. He explained that the element was not yet perfect, and that they should not even *consider* showing it.

To my dismay, they didn't.

In fact, Ren decided not to let me perform the loop again in public for another two years. So I continued, day after day, to do it 'twenty more times, flawlessly' in complete isolation.

After a solid performance in the Belorussian Championship, I was named for the Belorussian National Team. The Junior Team, actually, since I was twelve years old. I modestly kept silent about that little detail, but made sure that everyone in Grodno heard about the National Team part.

My next competition was the USSR Championship. By that time, my gymnastics arsenal included the back flip on the beam, the loop, and a few other incredibly difficult elements, many of which had never even been performed by male gymnasts. But Ren was still not ready to present these elements to the public. Perhaps he just wanted me to continue perfecting my skills, but my guess is that he didn't want to 'shoot sparrows with a cannon'.

So, during that meet, I performed rather trivial combinations, and didn't even place in the top three. During warm-ups, I even fell off the balance beam while doing an elementary split.

Just before my actual performance, Ren gave in.

'Okay,' he said. 'Include the flip in the beam routine.'

In practice, I had fallen many times while working on the flip, so I concentrated as hard as I could, and executed it perfectly. I was so pleased with myself that I went into my basic split – and tumbled right off the beam. So much for that.

Despite that mishap, I won a gold for the vault, and another for the uneven bars. My vault was rather ordinary, but the judges seemed to like it. The vault was named after Yamashita, a famous Japanese gymnast who had pioneered the move. The Yamashita vault consists of a beautiful, high first-flight phase, support (on the vault itself), 'bend-un-bend', and a second-flight phase. The jargon may sound confusing, but it looks pretty much the way it sounds.

Anyway, Ren changed the structure of the vault to a short, quick take-off from the beat board, followed by a push-off from the apparatus, and then a long, beautiful flight. This vault is no more difficult than the original Yamashita, but because of the novelty and the unexpected change in my profile, it was very flashy. I must have done it pretty well, because the other coaches looked at Ren approvingly.

Larissa Semyenovna Latynina, who was a famous ex-champion as well as the senior coach of the USSR Team, came over personally to give Ren her verdict. 'Your interpretation of the vault is very interesting,' she said to him, after congratulating me, 'but the first flight phase must be made longer.'

Ren shook his head. 'Impossible. That will reduce the post-flight.'

'It *must* be changed,' she said.

Ren shook his head more vehemently. 'No. Don't you see? The sum of moves will remain the same' (meaning, essentially, that some of my momentum would be wasted in the first flight) 'so the second flight will be affected.'

Latynina just sniffed, and walked away.

This was the first of many run-ins Ren and I were to have with the National Team leadership. Larissa Latynina was not just another coach; she was the highest official of the National Team. Her authority in the world of Soviet gymnastics was considered unimpeachable. Latynina subscribed to the old-school beliefs about the way the sport should be presented to the world. Her major theory was that it was easy to learn 'tricks', but that femininity and expressiveness were far more important. What she didn't seem to appreciate was the possibility that both of these goals could be achieved simultaneously. In her desire to maintain dominance in gymnastics, she wanted to prevent it advancing. Anyone involved with sport knows that improvements in techniques and broadening of horizons are what keep a sport exciting and alive.

Latynina also did not approve of gymnasts who were successful when they were 'too young'. And I certainly qualified on that count.

At the time, I had no idea how genuine a roadblock the National Team leadership would be to my gymnastics future.

The Rostov National Championship in 1969 was my last test before I joined the National Team at the age of fourteen. I was so busy working with Ren that I didn't have time to worry about my prospects. I figured that he was my coach and he knew what I should be doing, and when I should be doing it. When he declared I was ready in every way for Rostov, I did my best to ignore my doubts. I couldn't help being nervous because among my competitors at the meet would be all the Soviet champions from the 1968 Olympics: Petrick, Burda, Karasyova, Voronina and Tourischeva. I had never previously competed at that level.

My age was another problem. Rostov was considered an adult championship, so sixteen was the minimum entry age. Ren – who never before or after defended me, or helped to solve my personal problems – set out on this occasion to argue, cajole and bribe on my behalf.

When he returned, he had just one instruction. 'If anyone asks,' he said, 'tell them you are sixteen.'

I did, and was able to sneak into the event. Ren and I both agreed that I had a perfect right to violate the pointless rule barring younger girls from the competition.

It was at the Rostov Championship that Ren finally made up his mind that I should show the judges everything. He felt that it was time to unleash all our weapons. Our main targets were the audience and the judges, but Ren also wanted to impress, and maybe distress, the establishment known as the State Ministry of Sport and Physical Culture (Goskomsport). What made it interesting was that our weapons were loaded with a type of ammunition no one had ever seen before.

I have always flourished on audience reaction and applause, but in those days it was more important for me to be able to look over at my coach and see his eyes filled with quiet confidence. Ren's expression was my inspiration. With his support, I could do anything.

So, in my performances, I did the loop, the 'cut-off kip' on the bars, the back flip on the beam, and our version of the Yamashita vault. We had also added dozens of acrobatics to my floor exercise, in direct conflict with our country's conservative gymnastics traditions.

My style, too, was deliberately defiant. It was fast, sharp and brisk. This at a time when the prevailing sentiment was that women's gymnastics should be elegant, smooth and almost gentle. But Ren's approach to the sport was completely original.

He had studied ballet, African dance, and many other forms of rhythm and dance. He then incorporated these disciplines into his floor exercises. Using his vast knowledge of movement and physical grace, he helped me develop a style that was supple, but also swift and jazzy. The gymnastics specialists at Rostov were not only impressed by the acrobatic elements, but surprised and puzzled by the unconventional combination of classical ballet and African dance.

The quickest reaction to my performance came from the audience, who rewarded me with an ovation. Audience reactions are always sincere, for they are not bothered, as are the gymnastics powers-that-be, about the intricate traditions and unspoken rules of the sport.

There were many comments, especially in the media, about my smile. Ren *always* reminded me to smile, even when I was lying on the floor after a bad fall and wanted to do nothing but burst into tears.

'Smile all the time,' he would say. 'When approaching the apparatus, when performing the loop, during your dismount. Smile! Otherwise, the spectator will see how hard you're working, and the illusion will be lost.'

Recently, I saw a videotape of one of my long-since-forgotten routines on the bars, and re-experienced the unpleasant memory of a small break during my dismount. And yet, I saw that I was still smiling. It wasn't a weak, foolish smile, but the smile of someone who was enjoying herself. There may have been the slightest hint of irony, but on the whole, I looked very happy. It disturbs me to remember that Ren *trained* me to execute that smile, exactly as he would train me to do a new and difficult element. That smile took years of zealous work-outs. So, I guess that smile is really Ren's creation. But, if it is, why does it look so sincere? I really hope that the smile is one thing that is completely mine.

Strange, then, that when I tried to smile the same way off the podium, away from the gym, I could only seem to manage a sort of grimace. Just like Ren's.

During competitions, when I was getting ready for my turn, I would look over at him, and he would make a hideous face at me, like something out of a horror movie. He always looked so funny that I never had to worry about 'putting on' a smile. It came naturally.

At the Championship in Rostov, I was very aware of the contrast between the audience and the judges. Every time I moved to a different apparatus, I sensed the audience following me. It was the first time at any meet that I felt attention focused principally on me. I *liked* that feeling.

The judges, however, awarded me modest scores, and the audience booed and jeered at them. I was too young to understand that the judges were being unfair. I was just happy to have placed fifth at such a prestigious competition. I was a success! The best part was that because of those fine results, I was now a member of the National Team of the USSR.

When I got home after the competition, I walked – maybe even strutted – all over Grodno, wearing my 'CCCP' sweat-suit, which was only given to National Team members. I was very proud of myself.

Ren was less satisfied. He had been watching the judges, and knew that they had liked the routines done by the unfamiliar little girl from Grodno. They had smiled and exchanged comments during my performances. Why hadn't this been reflected in my scores?

At Rostov, and every other large event before the 1972 Munich Olympics, the *Sovietski Sport* newspaper would carry an article with a couple of paragraphs devoted to Ren and me. It would say something to the effect of 'Yesterday, during the warm-ups, O. Korbut from the city of Grodno demonstrated something awful which had nothing in keeping with the glorious traditions of the invincible Soviet gymnastics.' The article would conclude with the statement that the Soviet Union did not need this kind of gymnastics.

In the Soviet Union (I hope, now, that things really are beginning to change) the structure of power in non-sporting areas was reflected in sports as well. The *Sovietski Sport* was an official arm of the USSR Sports Committee. Any opinions expressed in its pages had been given official approval by the leaders of the Sports Committee. As a result, the Committee's prejudices would be imposed upon readers as 'facts'.

I can only imagine that the judges reasoned, 'Why should we put ourselves on the line if the Sports Committee bosses seem to think Korbut's style has no future?' I don't blame those judges because that's how our system worked and they were considered loyal and obedient servants of that system. By Western standards, their behaviour was inexcusable, but the unfortunate flaws of the world in which I grew up have to be recognized.

Back in 1969, of course, I was just happy to be on the National Team. I was not exactly spending my free time worrying about politics.

My next step would be to go to the National Team Training Camp in Leselidze. Leselidze is situated on the Black Sea, an area famous for its warm, sunny weather. The location would be pleasant, but my main priority was to prepare for the World Championships in Ljubljana.

When I got to Leselidze, I was delighted to lay on the beach, listening to the unfamiliar sound of waves lapping at my feet. I was welcomed by everyone, but the senior gymnasts seemed to be carefully scrutinizing the two newcomers to the team, Tanya Schegol'kova and me. The veterans would lie in the sun all day while the two of us would run off to work out. I couldn't understand why they never did anything, yet had still managed to become Olympic champions. No one bothered to tell me that the main purpose of our stay was rest and relaxation.

I had promised Ren that I would work out for six hours a day. I was convinced that the others must be geniuses, since they could afford to laze around, so I worked even harder, trying to catch up. I was still too inexperienced to know that the ability to turn energy on and off when needed is an indication of one's true talents.

I was on reasonably friendly terms with the other girls, but I had hoped to make lots of close friends right away. When I became a veteran myself, I understood their attitudes. New girls come to the team as your eventual replacements. In gymnastics, a five- or six-year competitive career is considered a long one. So, the footsteps echoing from behind sound especially loud.

Tamara Lazakovich was the most friendly, and mischievous, of the old girls. She was very much a corrupting influence, teaching the 'greenhorns' to smoke and drink.

'Let's have some wine,' she said one day when we were on our way to work out.

39

'What?' I was shocked. 'Before training? Besides, I'd rather have some ice cream.'

We came to two booths: one sold ice cream, the other wine. I watched in astonishment as Tamara helped herself to some of the wine. Then, half an hour later, I was even more horrified as I saw her sweating profusely and working on the beam. I still don't know how she kept from falling. As I got to know her better, I would be amazed to see her drink as much as a full bottle of cognac at night, and then perform perfectly the next morning.

I was finally making new friends, but I missed Ren. I missed his look, his advice, and even his eternal 'poorly done today, could be better' grumble. But I was on my own now, and Larissa Latynina, the senior coach, was the one giving me advice and instructions.

When I got back to Grodno, Ren could scarcely believe the change in me.

'What does that dancing mean?' he demanded during our first practice. 'Who taught you this?'

I stopped in confusion, not sure what he meant.

All his worst fears had come true. During my stay in Leselidze, I had acquired a new and faceless style of gymnastics. Detesting our impulsive, explosive method, Latynina had trained me in her own way. She did her best to adjust my performances to the stereotypes of 'victorious Soviet gymnastics' and the result was a crazy hodgepodge of contradictory elements.

'Why do you spread your fingers?' Ren shouted, as our work-out continued.

It was my friend Tamara Lazakovich who always spread her fingers. Like a sponge, I had absorbed that quirk without even realizing it.

'Why is one hand higher than the other?' he yelled. Lazakovich.

'And what's wrong with your head?' he asked indignantly. 'Why do you tilt it?'

Once again, Lazakovich.

'*Now* you're walking like a goose!' he said. 'Who is it this time?'

40

That time, it was just plain confusion.

From then on, Ren kept me hidden from prying eyes, and even insisted that I should not look at any television programmes about gymnastics. I was not supposed to watch other gymnasts during meets, and I was *definitely* not supposed to go back to Leselidze ever again.

'You'd be better off with no training at all than with that kind of training,' he said, huffily.

Of course, I had to attend the scheduled training periods, whether he liked it or not. Ren knew that it would be useless to talk to Latynina about the situation, so he made up his mind to accompany me, even if it meant paying all his own expenses.

In those days, we did not have video equipment, which now makes it possible to analyse your own work-out and correct your mistakes. So, you really *needed* the critical eye of a good coach. Once you repeat a wrong movement a few times, it is stored in your muscle memory and can slip out at any time. Sometimes, the movement will stay in your head, like an annoying tune, and interfere with your work for weeks.

Unfortunately, Ren could not accompany me on every trip to Leselidze. Officially, he was not permitted to come at all. Later, he was not allowed (officially) to participate at the Olympic Games or the World Championships. The Sports Committee considered him superfluous, and he was not sufficiently tactful or deferential to be able to plead his case and get them to lift the ban. Occasionally he managed to get permission to visit the city where a championship was being held and, once there, he would coach me from the stands. The whole situation was stupid and unfair.

The National Team went to Leselidze three or four times a year, and preparing for the World Meet was our main task. During that first year, I quickly got used to the idea of being a fully fledged member of the national squad. The team at the World Championships would have six members, and since I had placed fifth at the National Championships, I knew that I would be among them.

But I wasn't. When the list was posted, and my name wasn't on it, I went to Latynina in a panic.

'What about me?' I asked.

'Don't worry,' she said kindly. 'You're going to Ljubljana, too. We've placed you on reserve. It is a very responsible position, and a great honour.'

I was on the verge of tears. 'Why on reserve? I'm ready to *compete*!'

'There was a tough fight for the second reserve position,' Latynina said, trying to sidestep the issue. 'But there was no argument that you should take the first slot.'

I was still trying not to cry. 'But – you *know* I am prepared for the competition.'

'Yes, I do know that,' she said – and the subject was closed.

I would go to Ljubljana in the lowly position of a reserve. It was the gymnastics version of sitting on the bench.

I was crushed.

Chapter Five

Our national team had dominated the World Championships and Olympic Games for many years, and those easy triumphs made our sports authorities very complacent. If we were already winning everything, why should we try anything new? The Soviet style was considered the absolute ideal in the world of gymnastics. To me, this attitude just seemed to parrot the foolish notion that 'the Socialist system is the best, most humane, and most progressive in the world'. Anything unusual, individualized and showy, in or out of sport, was considered offensive.

There was another obstacle that prevented many talented gymnasts from joining the sport. In football or hockey, for example, if a non-Moscow team became a champion, the newspapers would immediately write about the crisis in Soviet football. Not Moscow football, *Soviet* football. It was very rare for non-Moscow residents to be invited to participate on national teams. The Sports Committee felt that 'provincials' need not apply.

I found out later that I was not the first of Ren's students whom the Moscow-controlled gymnastics machine tried to break. Elena Volchetskaya, who had taken pity and selected me many years before, had herself been a victim. Elena was a Master of the Sport, and after winning the USSR Cup, she had been taken to the Prague Championship as the number three athlete on the National Team. During her warm-ups, the audience response was so enthusiastic that the coaches (with typical stupidity) decided not to allow her to compete at all. The reason was simple: her style did not look 'Soviet' enough. The coaches also wanted one of their favoured athletes, Vera Caslavska, to win the championship, and with Elena out of the competition, Caslavska's chances would be greatly improved. Caslavska did, in fact, win at Prague that year.

So there was plenty of ugly precedents for my situation. I was probably lucky that I was even allowed to go to Ljubljana as a *reserve*.

Once there, I was given the peculiar role of serving as an advertising agent for the Soviet team. Usually, the day before the international meets, the jury of judges sits down and watches the reserve gymnasts perform, in order to agree their standards of evaluation for the real competition. It is a sort of rehearsal in objectivity.

During the reserve performance, I did all my routines casually and faultlessly, without bothering to include any superior difficulty tricks. Why bother? But even without them, the judges gave me very high scores, and I was the winner of the unofficial World Championship Among Reserve Team Members.

Big deal.

The next morning, one of our coaches, Taisiya Demidenko, came running up to me with the morning newspapers, and gave me a warm hug.

'Look,' she said happily. 'What nice publicity you've created! Now it will be much easier for the rest of us.'

The newspapers had all reported how well I had done, saying that one could only imagine how good the Soviet team was if they put gymnasts like Olga Korbut on *reserve*.

I was less than thrilled by this compliment.

I think the real reason they took me to Ljubljana was because during the Olympics in Mexico City, for the first time, the Soviet team had run into a few problems. The German team, led by Erika Zuchold and Karin Janz, had mounted a serious challenge and continued to do so at Ljubljana.

Fidgeting and agonizing, I wished our girls well, and silently protested Latynina's decision to put me on reserve. The German team was cutting into our concrete wall of conceit and conservatism, and our team's chance of victory was endangered. The GDR team was beginning to represent the new wave of gymnastics: unorthodox, refreshing and innovative. That would open the road to Munich for me.

When I got back to Grodno, I wept a little, complaining to Ren about the injustice of my reserve status.

'You have to keep working,' was all Ren said, with his usual dispassion. 'Here, I have a new element I think you will enjoy.'

Ren never wasted time complaining. He just did what he did best: work, and then work some more.

After our team's narrow victory in Ljubljana, the sports leadership began to worry. Soviet supremacy was under siege, and the thought of losing gold medals was hard for the coaches to stomach. Maybe it was time to make some changes.

The National Team was invited to go to Japan, and I was terribly excited. Japan was so far away, a land of marvel and magic. Normally, when athletes travel, they don't see much more than airports, hotel rooms and sports halls, but I vowed that my trip to Japan would be different. In my imagination, Japan was a glorious and mysterious place where there were geishas and samurais on the streets, where people ate with chopsticks, and drank sake all day long. I could hardly wait to get there and see it all for myself.

When we arrived in Nagoya, Tamara Lazakovich (my bad influence) and I checked into the hotel and then went out to find some night life. Before we got a hundred yards away from our hotel, we were already lost. There were neon signs everywhere, and thousands of cars, and it was like nothing we had ever seen in our lives. The streets all looked exactly alike, cluttered with little boutiques and shops, and for some reason, all of the cars seemed to be white Toyotas. We were completely and thoroughly lost – and starting to panic.

Then, I saw a policeman standing on a sidewalk. We were saved! Of course, I forgot that he wasn't going to be able to speak Russian, and we certainly couldn't speak Japanese. My command of English was limited to 'excuse me', 'I'm sorry', and 'thank you', so even if he spoke that language, we would still be lost.

Trying to be as polite as I could, I asked him in Russian, 'Comrade militiaman, pardon – policeman, would you be so kind as to tell us where our hotel is situated?' Then, I finished my plea in English, saying, 'Excuse me?' To drive my point home, I dangled my hotel key in front of his eyes.

I don't know if he mistook us for young foreign hookers inviting him to our room for some fun, but he just shook his head sternly and tapped his watch with his forefinger.

'No, excuse me?' I repeated in English.

He frowned.

After half an hour of trying to explain our desperate situation, Tamara and I both began sobbing. The police officer frowned again, glanced at his watch, then grabbed our hands decisively and began hauling us off.

Tamara and I looked at each other with the same terrible thought in our minds: what if he was arresting us?

He took us about a hundred yards, then through an underground passage, and when we emerged, we were standing in front of our hotel. Our gratitude knew no bounds, but I think our stream of Russian thank-yous was lost on him.

Our coaches and chaperones were furious, and lectured us at length. How dare we get lost in a capitalist country, full of CIA agents with their provocative tricks and schemes? Tamara and I believed every bit of this harangue, even though it didn't exactly square with the kind police officer who had left his post to help us.

For the rest of our tour, we didn't stray more than three steps away from the rest of the group. We were worried about the unknown 'schemes of the CIA agents', but we were also afraid that if we got lost again, we would not be lucky enough to find *another* kind capitalist policeman.

Japan remains the brightest memory of my childhood. Everything was unusual there: clothes, architecture, traditions and lifestyle. We did, however, have some bad luck with the food. At one reception, we adventurously grabbed chopsticks instead of forks – and went home hungry. Another time, we got food poisoning after devouring a mountain of oysters. A third time, we helped ourselves to hearty portions of some delicious chicken, only to learn later that it was either frog or snake. At least half of the team immediately got sick.

This was my first trip to a 'Western' country, and I was amazed when I saw a toyshop. Whenever we had spare time to go sightseeing, I would spend it with my nose pressed up against toyshop windows. Growing up in a poverty-stricken family, I had never had, or even seen, toys. On subsequent trips abroad, I always went out of my way to find toyshops.

In Japan, I spent hours on end transfixed by a picture of a red rubber octopus climbing a wall. I loved the funny electronic walrus trying to get out of an aquarium, and the little torpedo-launching submarine. There were dolls which could speak, dance, cry and laugh – just like real people. My favourites though, were the trick toys, like a jack-in-the-box, a laughing bag, and a fake fly in fried eggs. We were given some per diem money, and I spent it all on toys. Once I got back to Grodno, I devoted a whole month to playing practical jokes on people. My family, of course, bore the brunt of this.

All this was exhilarating for me because, once I had been accepted at the sports school, my childhood had ended. I never had the chance to go to a school dance, or a New Year's party. Nor was I allowed to get acquainted with boys. Ren didn't want me to expend a morsel of energy on anything other than gymnastics. Even my academic progress was completely irrelevant to him. Only gymnastics mattered, and consequently my life was rather one-dimensional.

While in Japan, we trained with Japanese gymnasts and shared our experiences. I was amazed by the scrupulous and painstaking attitude of the Japanese gymnasts each time they performed their routines during work-outs – the absolute precision that was the hallmark of their style.

We found one aspect of Japanese athletic life very difficult. They worked out in cool, well-ventilated gymnasiums, and we were always freezing. We tried to stay warm by wearing coats and blankets, and would sit next to the heaters between routines. Later, we learned that the Japanese athletes would rub themselves with special warming ointments in the locker room before practice, and then go out to the cool, invigorating gym. That explained a lot, but we were still cold.

I worked as hard as any of my team-mates on the Japanese tour, but there were still no guarantees that the doors to the National Team would be open to me. The outcome of the USSR Championship would determine the final composition of the team for the 1972 Olympics. It didn't seem likely that I would be allowed to be a member of that prestigious group, and I hated the idea of remaining a reserve.

During the warm-up meets for the Championship, I fell from the various apparatuses as often as anyone else did, which was disappointing because that resulted in deductions from my precious scores. At each meet, I invariably received the prize for 'Originality and Complexity of Combinations', but that was of little consolation. The cliché in the Soviet newspapers was, 'Tourischeva lives to win; Korbut – to amaze.' That wasn't enough; I wanted to *win*.

I probably should have slowed down, and taken the necessary time to master each new movement, but at training sessions we just kept devising even newer ones. I had great confidence in Ren's ability as a coach, and did whatever he told me.

When I could not execute a new element after a hundred attempts, I would despair. 'Why do we need it?' I would complain. 'Other girls have normal programmes – why do *we* have to stick out?'

'Because you can do things nobody ever did before,' Ren would answer calmly.

But I was not placated that easily. 'What good does it do? I only get deductions!'

Ren would just shrug. 'The deductions are not important at all. It doesn't matter whether you become a champion or not. What *matters* is that you overturn the entire gymnastics world.'

What mattered to me was that the other girls on the National Team seemed to be laughing at me. Their programmes were five times easier than mine, but they would receive much higher marks. I wanted those high marks, too.

But if I kept arguing, Ren would just leave the gym.

'Think about your behaviour, Olga,' he would say, and the door lock would click behind him. Basically, I knew that he was right. It was boring to polish the same element by doing it a thousand times, but it was necessary.

I think it was then, at the beginning of 1972, that I gave up playing at gymnastics. I now wanted to set specific goals for myself, and accomplish them. I stopped being mere material in my coach's hands, and started working for *myself*. If I hadn't thought about the danger of falling during the loop before, I now took the risk of breaking my spine quite seriously. I had to be smart, and learn how to do everything correctly. There was no room for mistakes.

I sensed that Ren silently applauded me, but his attitude did not change. If anything, he became even stricter with me. The difference was that now I was more likely to pay attention.

I think the invention of foam rubber may have done more than anything else to revolutionize gymnastics. I would be standing in front of the vaulting horse, preparing to do a complicated pirouette before pushing off, followed by another pirouette during the second-flight phase. If I hesitated too long, Ren would understand and lower the horse into a pit lined with foam rubber. I would do the move 'twenty times, flawlessly', and then the horse would be moved up a couple of inches, foam rubber still everywhere. This would continue 'twenty times, flawlessly' until the horse had reached its normal position, and all the mats were gone. But if they hadn't been there in the first place, I might never have had the courage to attempt, let alone perfect, some of my riskier moves.

During this period I really enjoyed our training sessions. We were getting ready for the Kiev USSR Championship in April, and the Moscow USSR Cup in July. After that, the six gymnasts who were going to Munich would be named.

Tourischeva and Lazakovich would definitely be two of the six, which meant that there were only four remaining spots available.

Ren started cutting the pauses from each of my exercises, and replacing them with transfers, which I thought were more difficult than the elements themselves. Nevertheless I learned them, and each exercise slowly grew from a set of innovative elements to a smooth, fully realized composition.

There are three basic components in gymnastics: strength, flexibility and choreography. It is important to note that choreography should *not* be ballet. It is far more athletic than that. Women's gymnastics, of course, has four apparatuses: the balance beam, the uneven parallel bars, the vault and the floor exercise. It is said that if you can do the beam successfully, you will become an Olympic champion . . . as long as you don't fall. Mastery of the horse takes on the same importance in men's gymnastics.

The beam is very tricky. Today, the beam is made of a softer, almost spongy, material, but it used to be wooden. It is not nearly as hard to work on the new one. Back flips are *much* easier to do on the spongy beam. The odd thing is that I was always most afraid of doing simple turns. I could do everything else fine – even the most difficult elements – but I was always scared when it was time to turn around.

The uneven bars became my favourite apparatus because I really felt as if I was flying. I also think the bars are the most beautiful of the four categories. The vault is tough because everything goes so fast, but you have to work hard on every single detail. It probably looks easier than some of the other apparatuses because it is over in the blink of an eye.

In the floor exercise, you can show everything that you know how to do. But, in addition to your skills, you are also trying to show who you are as a person. Because of this, it is very important to find exactly the right piece of music: one that fits your personality perfectly. The wrong music can ruin the routines of even the most gifted gymnasts.

My gymnastics arsenal for the Munich Olympics was full of elements nobody else had ever done. On the beam, in addition to my back flip, I was doing a back lay-out dive through a chest roll. We moved the back somersault to the end of the exercise, because if I did it earlier, everything that followed was an anticlimax. As it was, the difficulty would increase gradually during the exercise, culminating in the startling flip.

Ren and I had worked endlessly on my Yamashita vault until we developed an even more extravagant variation. On the bars I had my loop, and in the floor exercise I was doing dives and chest rolls and a lot of other brand-new moves. Ren and I completely discarded traditions when we designed my programme. We knew that my routines had been perfectly polished, and our goal now was to try to electrify the judges, along with the crowds.

I felt quite light-hearted at the USSR Championship in Kiev. I had worked as hard as humanly possible, was prepared to do my best – and the rest was beyond my control.

Andrei Voznesenski, a famous Russian poet, wrote an article about me in *Komosolskaya Pravda*, a national newspaper put out by the Young Communist League. The title of the article was 'Do Not Forbid Olga to Fly!' It was the first time an article had ever been written *supporting* me. Maybe the tide was beginning to turn.

I won the bronze medal in the individual combined events competition, but if the audience had been the judge, I would have taken the gold. I agreed with Ren that I should, above all, perform for the spectators, but I wanted the same amount of official recognition as well. I guess I'm the kind of person who can slave away at routine work six days a week, but needs to be told 'thank you' on the seventh.

I got my 'thank you' three months later, when I won the USSR Cup. After that, the final composition of the Olympic Team was announced: Tourischeva, Lazakovich, Burda, Saadi, Koshel, and Korbut.

I was on my way to the Olympics!

51

Chapter Six

Before going to Munich, Ren and I discarded my routines and started from scratch. If we broke them down to the very basics, we could do still more polishing and refining. Now that I had won an important gold medal, I would no longer be satisfied with anything less than that.

We had the most doubts about my floor exercise. The music we were using was 'Flight of the Bumblebee', and we had exhaustively choreographed the entire routine. As soon as audiences heard the first bars of the famous tune, they would explode into applause, which then died instantly as they concentrated on the show. A fleet-footed, impetuous bee-girl darted out on to the mat and dashed from one imaginary flower to another, enjoying the sun, the blue sky, life, and her free flight. When the little bee came to a halt, the audience always responded with thunderous applause.

I loved the bee routine, but the judges had never given me a mark higher than 9.60. At Kiev, the jury, without hesitation, had awarded me a 9.55, ignoring the booing from the crowd. At Munich, I had to do better than that.

Tourischeva and Lazakovich were the queens of the floor exercise, and my composition was not considered sufficiently elegant or feminine. People also felt that I was still too short to do true justice to the gentle grace of the floor exercise. The sports authorities were resigned to accepting my work on the other apparatuses, but they would not tolerate my aggressive innovations in the floor exercise.

A month before the Munich Games, the National Team moved to Minsk to train at the Palace of Sports. Working out at the Palace was considered good luck. The facilities were wonderful, and Ren and I were provided with a choreographer, a private accompanist and everything else we wanted. We believed that, armed with riches like these, we could accomplish anything.

We spent the bulk of our time working on the 'Bumblebee'. Even with experts all around him, Ren would personally demonstrate what he wanted me to do. His clumsy efforts were always right on target, and his caricatures of my mistakes were vividly imprinted in my mind. I would not make those mistakes again.

At the end of July, we had a final team rehearsal, in front of a packed house. Everything was real, except for the scores. They were not announced, but merely recorded in the notepads of the team coaches. Afterwards, they would decide among themselves how to rank each of the team members, and decide upon the order of competition.

Ren and I still weren't happy with the 'Bumblebee'. Then, something happened that confirmed our reputation among the National Team of being thoroughly unreliable and irresponsible. It was our last day there, and we were having lunch at the restaurant in the Yubileynaya Hotel. During the meal, records were played for background music, and Ren and I suddenly heard a wonderful tune. I didn't know its title or author, but we both stopped chewing and looked at each other. The music went through me like an electric shock. Why should I do the 'Bumblebee'? I didn't need classical music; I needed this unknown 'ta-daram, tadaram, tadaram!'

Seconds later, our lunch forgotten, we were begging the manager of the restaurant to let us have the record.

Poor Evsei Vevrick, our accompanist. He was offended to the very roots of his soul by our request to drop the 'Bumblebee'. It is insanity to change a perfected combination, where every move is coordinated with every sound, *especially* at the last minute. But, Ren and I loved that unknown melody, and dubbed it 'Mischievous Girl'.

The new composition retained a lot of 'Bumblebee' movements, but the fresh music filled them with another meaning, taste, scent and colour. A brand-new character appeared. Mischief, cunning, delight, playfulness, joy, unexpectedness, childish coquetry – it was all there. It was as though the music had been written with me in mind.

Ren had to shoulder the storm of outrage from the team leaders. I merely felt the echoes and, in any case, was deaf to reproaches – simply happy at last to have found the right song.

Immediately before I started packing to go to Munich, there was a potentially disastrous incident. One of our accompanists, Kokovina, found 150 roubles missing from her purse. That was a great deal of money in those days – about a month's salary. I was sorry about the theft, but forgot about the whole thing once it had been reported to the militia.

Then, one day, during a work-out, Latynina came to Ren, and confided that she had some very bad news.

'What's happened?' Ren asked.

'Part of the stolen money has been found,' she whispered.

'Well, great,' Ren said. 'Why is that bad news?'

Latynina lowered her voice even more. 'Fifty roubles were found in Olga's hotel room between the wall and the bed. Do you realize what that means?'

The insinuation made Ren very angry. 'She couldn't have done it,' he said.

'Then, where did the money come from?' Latynina asked.

Ren turned to me, raising his voice. 'Olga, you go on training. I'll be back soon.'

I continued what I was doing, wondering why he looked so upset.

Ren and Latynina went to my hotel room, and when Ren saw the two twenty-five-rouble notes, his blood ran cold. He did not believe the accusation, but he knew that anyone suspected of theft would be banished from the Olympic Team. He picked up the phone and called German Bokun, the then Deputy Chairman of the Belorussian Sports Committee.

'Don't touch anything,' Bokun said. 'I'll find a good investigator and he'll be there soon.'

Moments later, the militia arrived. They took fingerprints, inspected the room, and questioned various people. I did not find out about any of this until the militia interrogated me. I was horrified and disgusted. Who would do such a thing to me?

A few days passed, and we heard that a thief had been arrested, but we never found out who it was, or who had *really* planted that money behind my bed.

Years before, the same sort of thing had happened to Ren's star pupil, Elena Volchetskaya, but in her case, it was food coupons instead of money. Every coupon bears the name of the competitor to whom it was issued. Elena had been in a canteen, given the barmaid a coupon, and it was marked with another name. Someone had slipped them to her just before one of the World Championship meets.

Immediately, an investigation was started. Elena was advised to confess, and told that she would then be forgiven. Ren wasn't with her, and she didn't know what to do, so she lied and said that she had stolen the coupons.

The 'forgiveness' she received was to be disqualified from competition for two years, and kicked off the National Team.

I don't know who did these things to us, but the why is obvious. Elena and I were both very young, and didn't realize that our smart and experienced colleagues were capable of such dirty tricks. There were stories about talented gymnasts who had missed important events due to acute and incomprehensible stomach disorders. And then, later, cleaning women would find empty laxative packages in hotel corridors, the contents having been given to the unsuspecting victims.

This happened not only to Ren's pupils, but to many others who made 'too much' progress 'too fast'. People are told about the spirit of friendship and comradeship among members of the USSR National Teams, but the truth is not always that pretty. Maybe in other sports, where team, rather than individual, efforts are required, true friendship is possible, but in gymnastics, we were a team only in the course of team competitions. During individual events, everyone would struggle to get her own medal, and we became bitter rivals. We would say hello when we met, but there were no real friendships.

Six of us went to Munich. Who were the other five? I will try to describe them, although in all honesty, I was so busy with my gymnastics and Ren that I paid very little attention to anything, or anyone, else during that period.

Ludmilla Tourischeva was considered a great gymnast, and she was a typical example of old-style gymnastics, except that she wasn't very graceful. She would compensate for that by working tirelessly. The result was secure, reliable, convincing and risk-free routines. This appealed to judges, who wanted everything to be 'right'.

Then, there was Tonya Koshel. She might not have been selected if the pre-Olympic training period had been held somewhere else, but it was in Minsk, the capital of Belorussia, and Tonya is Belorussian. She was a tough and reliable competitor. She would always go first in competitions, and everything depended on her. If the first team member falls off an apparatus, then the tone is set, and the others tend to start 'dropping off' like ripe apples from a tree. Tonya was a good choice to be first, because she was always very dependable.

Luba Burda was a remarkably gifted gymnast, and, in my opinion, her coach, Shtukmann, was a genius. I believe he is the only coach, other than Ren, to have changed the course of Soviet – and therefore, international – gymnastics. Luba was much more gifted than myself. She could learn a new element during two or three work-outs, but she was not patient enough to make her performance really secure. Shtukmann's only flaw was that he let her get away with such laziness. Otherwise, I think she would have achieved much more.

Tamara Lazakovich was a terrific worker. Sometimes, I thought she worked twenty-five hours a day. In any condition (even with a hang-over), at a competition of any calibre, she was a fierce fighter.

Elvira Saadi attempted nothing new in her routines, but what she did, she did beautifully. However, she was never really able to challenge her team-mates. She was a very nice person, and I always loved talking to her. Maybe it's easier to become friends when there is no rivalry, but she was the only person on the team with whom I felt genuinely at ease.

I'm sure that none of those evaluations are completely objective, but they are my true opinions. That is how I really felt about the five gymnasts who accompanied me to Munich.

Sometimes I wonder, was that girl *really* me, in Munich's Sportshalle in 1972? Time has worn the colours, dulled the feelings, and made it all seem so distant. It was only a year ago that I first saw myself perform on tape – *ever*! I watched my performance there with a feeling of disbelief and cautious doubt. How could that seventeen-year-old girl with the huge bows be *me*? I wish I had seen the tapes twenty years earlier, when they would have seemed more familiar to me. But, in all that time, they never showed my films in the Soviet Union. Ludmilla Tourischeva was a member in good standing of the Communist Youth Organization, so they would show her instead, as though I didn't even exist. Twenty years.

My biggest worry as we got ready to depart for West Germany was whether I would be prepared psychologically for the pressures of Olympic competition. If only I had participated in at least *one* major international competition before Munich. Then, maybe, I would have felt more confident. My major emotions, the night before we left, were fear and anxiety. For days, I had been thinking – constantly, obsessively – about the Olympics. What would it be like there, and how would I do?

'With such nerves, you'd lose to any first-grader in our school,' Ren told me.

I had no real answer for that.

'Maybe you shouldn't go?' he suggested, with his usual sense of devil.

That remark struck even more of a bullseye than he had probably intended.

'You – you're a despot!' I said, stuttering in my fury. 'A tyrant! Look at the palms of my hands!' I can't go out anywhere. I'm ashamed of the callouses. Do these look like a *girl's* hands? I'm tired. I can't do it anymore. I've *had* it with gymnastics.'

Three time Olympic Champion Olga Korbut in 1972.

Olympic gymnastics champion Olga Korbut and musical star Leonid Bortkevich exchange wedding rings in 1978.

Olga Korbut riding at a training session in 1983.

Olga Korbut performing in November 1975.

Ren listened attentively to my tirade.

'Good,' he said, when I was finished. 'Now, you're better.'

I actually *did* feel better. Yelling at him had been like opening a pressure valve and letting everything stream out. Just like that, my nerves were gone.

'And now,' Ren said calmly, 'let's get down to business.'

I nodded, as he began giving me instructions about my training programme, as though I were just going on a little trip to Leselidze.

'Don't think about the competition, just work, Olga,' he said. 'Work as usual. But work *consciously*. Think about what you are doing. I won't be nearby, so nobody is going to point out your mistakes. If something goes wrong, don't panic. Just think it over, and try to find an answer. You are no longer a pupil.'

I nodded, my hands pressed tightly together in my lap. He was not going to Munich with me because the Sports Committee had not put him on the list of officials accompanying the team. And it still wasn't clear if he would be allowed to go as a tourist. So, I would probably be alone, even though I needed him there. Needed his eyes watching me, recharging me, like a solar battery drawing energy from the sun.

'If you make the same mistake twice, switch over to another apparatus,' he advised. 'And switch your mind over, too. Don't be lazy during warm-ups – show them everything. Give them the somersault, the loop, the whole works.'

I frowned. 'What for? Why waste the energy?'

'It's not a waste,' he said. 'Judges there don't read Soviet newspapers, so their minds will be more open. If they like you during warm-ups, it will be easier for them to give you unbiased scores later.'

That made sense, and I nodded.

'You're going to be fine,' Ren said. 'You're in excellent condition, and you can do anything. You are the best gymnast in the world, Olga. And your gymnastics is the future of gymnastics.'

These were, by no means, the sorts of remarks Ren usually made. '*Our* gymnastics, Renald,' I corrected him.

'Well,' he said, and shrugged. 'Show them what you can do, as if it were just a work-out.'

As usual, he did not mention medals. To Ren, gymnastics was hard work, and nothing else.

I did not want to be in Munich without him.

The team arrived in West Germany a week before the competitions started. Immediately, we were plunged into a festive atmosphere of joy, anxiety and excitement. Our coaches kept us segregated from obtrusive journalists, warning that reporters would stop at nothing in their attempts to 'interrogate' us.

At that point in the Games, I think our coaches may have been right to keep us isolated, so that none of us would lose our heads and start flourishing on fame we hadn't yet earned. But later on, this isolation was to hurt us.

Using a notebook filled with Ren's detailed instructions, I applied myself as diligently as ever to my work. The programme he had given me was even more intense than usual. I tried to concentrate solely on working out, but when I took time to listen to German radio, I would hear the name 'Korbut' being mentioned more and more often. I didn't speak the language, so I wasn't sure what they were saying about me, but it must have been pretty good.

Following Ren's advice, I did my best during the warm-ups, showing nearly everything I could do. After each apparatus, I would try to gauge the audience's reaction. It was, increasingly, a strong, positive one. I had no way of finding out, but I couldn't help wondering what the judges were secretly scratching down in their little notepads. I also wondered if I should have followed the strategy that the famous Czech gymnast, Vera Caslavska, had used in the past. She would show one programme during warm-up, and perform a completely different one at the competitions. People were amazed and fascinated by her versatility, and it gave her an extra advantage. Maybe I should have done that, or maybe I should have tried to, but I knew it was too late to change my mind about *anything*. The gymnastics competition was to begin the next day.

I was as ready as I would ever be.

Chapter Seven

Larissa Latynina and Yuri Titov, the chairman of the Gymnastics Federation, gathered the team together, and spoke to us about what lay ahead. Their final words were: 'We believe, we hope, we expect.'

At least they weren't putting any pressure on us.

What could they really say in a situation like that? We all knew what was expected of us. And, anyway, things had improved since the old days. Elena Volchetskaya had been forced to make a written promise before she was allowed to go to a World Championship, saying, 'I, Elena Volchetskaya, pledge to place at least third.'

That night, I saw Ren, who had managed to get permission to come as a tourist after all. The hotel he was staying at was ten miles away, and with all of the traffic, it took him one and a half hours to get to the Olympic Village. Once he arrived, he was not allowed in because of all the rigid security measures. Unfortunately, Ren was considered 'unauthorized' personnel.

He waited at the gates for almost two hours, hoping to see me go by. Then he saw Tamara Lazaokovich, who passed the message along, but when I got to the gates, he wasn't there. Realizing that I had fallen for another of her stupid practical jokes, I turned to leave.

'Hey, Olga! Korbut!' a familiar voice yelled after me. 'Where do you think you're going?'

The shouts came from an imposing gentleman wearing a dark trenchcoat and a wide-brimmed felt hat. I had never seen Ren wearing *anything* other than an old sweatsuit and Czech half-shoes, so I hadn't recognized him.

When we finally stopped laughing, I gave him detailed reports about my work-outs.

'My uneven bars are fine,' I said, 'but I'm afraid of doing the somersault on the beam, and my heels hurt very badly.'

'Look what a nice suit I've bought!' He stood there, admiring himself. 'I have never in my life had anything like this.'

That seemed like idle chatter, and I ignored it. 'The German girls look very tough to beat,' I went on. 'I especially like Janz.'

He ignored that. 'Have you seen the local buses?' he asked. 'Wow! Double-deckers. Can you imagine such a thing?'

At first, I was annoyed, but then, I began to relax and chatted with him happily about his fancy suit and hat, public transportation, and other pleasantly mundane topics.

He didn't mention gymnastics until just before he left.

'Remember, Olga,' he used his fingers to pull his mouth into a hideous grimace. 'Don't forget to *smile*.'

Right.

Over the next few days, we would go through all three sets of competition: the team, the all-round and the individual events.

The crowd was great, and I quickly warmed to its attention and admiration. I had always heard that Germans were a cool, restrained and disciplined people, but after each successfully executed element, the Munich Sportshalle would explode into an ovation, complete with shouts and whistles. When I only received a 9.60 for my beam routine – including the still-unprecedented back flip – the hurricane of catcalls and boos from the audience threatened to bring the place tumbling down.

After the optional programme, I was carried away by the applause, hearing an ocean of voices roaring, 'Ol-ga! Ol-ga! Ol-ga!' It was a wonderful feeling; one of the best I have ever experienced. At home, in the Soviet Union, the crowds had always been much quieter, with no real emotional connection between athlete and audience. Probably they were too shy and constrained to express their feelings openly and sincerely. Either way, I loved the overwhelming response I was receiving in Munich.

I loved it when a severe policeman at the Olympic Village gates did not wait until I found my pass, just giving me a broad grin and waving me through, greeting me as 'Fräulein Korbut'. I loved making my way through admiring throngs and signing their autograph books. It was amazing – one day, I was nobody, and the next day, I was a *star*. It was almost more than I could take in.

All my fears were gone, and I was happy to go out and jump and dance and tumble for my beloved audience. But sports and injuries go hand in hand. Instead of pleasure, I suddenly felt an acute backache. My joy was now mingled with sharp, piercing pain.

In the team competition, I was in third place, behind my team-mate Tourischeva and Karin Janz from Germany. But we were only 0.15 points apart. Close enough? Too far? There was no way to know.

Then, it was time for my floor exercise. The 'Bumblebee' had transformed itself into the 'Mischievous Girl'. As I performed, I forgot about everything except my childhood. There was no tournament, no pressure, no anything. I felt I was playing alone in a beautiful meadow. It was just fabulous.

But my back still hurt.

The scores were up. 9.80. So, dear Larissa Latynina, I'm not the floor exercise type, right?

Now the vault. The Yamashita she disliked so much. 9.65? After *that*? The judges were not exactly the most generous in the world. But no matter. I just wanted my back to stop hurting.

I had a lead (and a good one) over Tourischeva and Janz. Great! Even though I no longer had the strength to tolerate the pain.

Finally, I had to stop attending my work-outs. I collapsed on my bed, feeling as though it would take a crane to lift me to my feet. I was only seventeen years old, and I was afraid. What was wrong with me? What if it was serious?

Moreover, I had ugly, incontrovertible proof that the friendship among Soviet team members did not extend beyond the propaganda. I had missed work-outs for two days straight, and not a single team-mate or coach had come to check on me. The excitement I had felt after all those ovations had acted like some sort of painkiller, but it had long since worn off.

On the third day, I knew I really could not get up without someone helping me, and no one was there. I missed yet another work-out and nobody bothered to come to my room to see if anything was wrong. I guess it was because the team competition was over. We had won, and now they didn't need me anymore. Maybe they were even *glad* that I had dropped out of sight, because now they would have a better chance to win individual medals.

Unknown to me, however, Ren was deeply concerned. He couldn't believe that his disciplined Olga would skip work-outs, but since he couldn't get into the Olympic Village, he had no way of finding out what was wrong. Finally, he was able, through some of the other athletes, to summon me to the gate. I dragged myself outside and over to the fence.

He stared at me. 'Olga! What happened to you?'

'My back hurts,' I mumbled.

Within a couple of minutes, Ren had managed to raise utter hell and bring the matter to everyone's attention.

'What's going on here?' he shouted. 'Someone gets sick in the Olympic Village, which is full of medical equipment and excellent doctors, and nobody cares! What's the matter with all of you?'

Now, three days too late, Latynina panicked, assistant coach Astakhova panicked, and the doctors came to give me a huge dose of novocaine. The pain went away, but the feeling that I was missing half of my back was very unpleasant. I didn't want to move, I didn't want to work-out, and I had *no* desire to smile.

'Olga, go to the bars!' Ren ordered.

'I can't,' I said unhappily. 'We were warned that if we went to the gym during the time allocated to others, we would be disqualified.'

But Ren insisted. 'Olga, if you don't warm-up on the bars now, you won't be able to compete,' he said. 'The muscles retain the memory of pain, and won't allow you to perform normally. Please, go! There's nobody in the gym now, and I'll be watching out.'

I knew he was right. I approached the gym, expecting the vicious bite of pain the first time I made a wrong move. But I couldn't risk going inside. I wouldn't be able to handle being disqualified. So, I hid around a corner, out of Ren's view. I don't think he ever knew.

When it was time to compete again, I ran to the apparatus, feeling no pain. The crowd was applauding, and chanting, 'Olga! Ol-ga!' Thank you, crowd. Oh, right – smile! I gave them my smile, hoping they knew how happy I was to see them all again.

Now, though, I had to concentrate on the bars. As I began, I suddenly realized how very right Ren had been. I *should* have come to the apparatus at least once to practise. Now I felt everything was wrong. Strange.

I was doing a very simple element, one I had performed thousands of times; one any schoolgirl at the Red Banner School could do with ease: the pike. I flew off the top bar, hitting the mattings below with my nose.

After that, I don't remember anything. I know I stood up, and mounted the bars again. I did a perfect loop, but it couldn't save the situation. For a fall, judges deducted not 0.50, as they do today, but 1.00. Then I fell again! Another simple move any kid could manage after a year of training.

Automatically, I mounted the bars once again, and continued my routine. I did it without conscious thought, so I guess it was just the internal memory of well-trained muscles.

When my routine was over, the only thing I recall is silence. I don't even remember when I started crying. It might have been after I dismounted the bars, or maybe it was after my beam routine, for which I was given an incredibly high (for those days) score of 9.90. I think it was after the beam. The truth is, I don't remember crying at all, but the photographic evidence I saw later is impossible to deny.

I felt as though my life was over.

They say that I was weeping, surrounded by reporters who took picture after picture, while Erika Zuchold and coach Astakhova were hugging and trying to console me. They say that the crowd was stunned into silence, then gave me a huge ovation – probably trying to cheer me up. The only thing imprinted in my mind is my score: 7.50. All my hopes and dreams of glory had been destroyed.

The only good thing is that I completely forgot about my back.

The next thing I remember is lying on the bed in my room. It was dark outside, and two words were pounding themselves into my brain over and over again – I lost. I lost. I lost. All night long, I had the same nightmare. Ren, looking at me reproachfully, saying, 'I had put all of my hopes on you. I didn't know you were such a – a –' Then he just shook his head, and left in disgust.

I got up more than once in the night to take a sleeping pill, and when I finally managed to open my eyes the next morning, my first waking thoughts were of the previous day's misery. I would have to hide myself somewhere, away from everybody – Ren, Latynina, the team, my former fans. If only I could be back in Grodno, where my mother would understand how awful I felt, and take care of me. How would I ever be able to live through this? I had let everyone down. I was a failure.

My team-mate, Tonya Koshel, burst into the room. 'Olga, are you still in bed?' she said, looking surprised. 'Renald Ivanovich is waiting for you.'

Oh, no! Oh, help! I wanted him to leave, but I just mumbled, 'All right, I'm coming.'

I didn't exactly hurry. I began to tidy up the already neat room, taking things out of my suitcase, only to return them again. I washed my face and combed my hair, *very slowly*. It was a five-minute walk to the gates, but it took me at least fifteen. I felt as if I was going to my execution.

Ren was standing on the other side of the fence, smiling.

'Olga, what's wrong?' he asked. 'Are you disappointed?'

I hung my head, his cheery mood making me feel even worse. How he must pity me today.

'Well, naturally you are,' he said. 'But, is the Olympiad over? Don't you want to try and get a couple of golds?'

'You'd better swear at me,' I said without lifting my head.

He frowned. 'What for?'

Was he kidding? 'For yesterday's performance,' I said.

'Why?' he said, shrugging. 'I came to praise you, not to curse.'

What? I looked up. 'Praise me?'

He smiled at me. 'Don't you know you're a top star now? Everybody is speaking only about you. I, myself, will soon be calling you "Olga Korbut".'

Top star? After yesterday? Not likely. 'Oh, sure,' I said.

'Fräulein Korbut,' he said, looking very stern, 'it is not befitting an Honoured Master of Sports to go to pieces. Come on, pull yourself together!'

Had he just said what I thought he said? 'A . . . Master?' I repeated dumbly.

He nodded. 'H-o-n-o-u-r-e-d. Congratulations!'

It didn't make any sense. Why would they give me the title 'Honoured Master of Sports' after yesterday's shameful effort? I should be *punished*, not rewarded.

'Anyway, time to get back to work,' Ren said, and started explaining to me, step by step, move by move, everything I should do at the finals in the individual events.

I nodded, repeating his instructions word for word as he gave them to me, surprised that this conversation – and my voice – sounded so very normal. As though yesterday was a long distant memory.

Onward and upward, I guess.

Once again, I was only able to fall asleep after taking a large dose of sleeping pills. I had nightmares, but not as many as I had had on the previous night.

My shadow, not me, showed up at the gym for an early work-out, knees shaking, head dizzy, feeling very weak. Because of the sleeping pills, my blood pressure was so low that I could not find the energy to mount the apparatus. My nightmare came back to me – falling, time after time, no matter what I did.

Somehow, I summoned all my strength and threw myself on to the damned uneven bars, forcing my mind to blot out the dream. This was my favourite apparatus. How could I have failed on it? But little by little, my confidence came back, and by the end of the work-out, I felt like myself again. On the same bars where I had – but, I wasn't going to think about that anymore. It was forgotten.

When the work-out was over, Larissa Latynina took me to the mess hall, and made me eat a piece of meat, with potatoes and some caviar. The food made me feel a little better, too.

A few hours later, it was the last evening of the gymnastics Olympiad. Four finals – one for each apparatus. The compulsory and optional scores would determine the final results. Luckily, the results of the team competition, when I had messed things up, would not affect the individual events competition. Unless, of course, I fell again. But I had put that out of my mind, right?

I have no idea how the audience greeted me that night because I didn't hear them. I didn't hear anything. I saw faces, and figures, but they didn't mean anything to me.

When it was time for me to do the bars, I didn't even hear my name announced and Astakhova had to push me in the direction of the apparatus before I moved towards the podium. I dipped my fingers into chalk, and licked the fingertips. Damn – I hadn't licked the right hand the way I should have. The way I usually did. A bad omen. So I returned to the chalk bowl and did it again, correctly.

Then I couldn't remember what to do next. I couldn't remember how my routine started! No, wait, wasn't it the pike, from which I had fallen? Yes! Maybe. I think so. Let's go!

The next thing I remember is landing after my dismount, knee-deep in the matting. Apparently it was over. What a relief! How had I done? My mind was a blank.

The judges gave me a 9.85. That was certainly a lot better than the 7.50, but my routine had been perfect, and the crowd wanted more. They shouted and cheered and stamped their feet until the Games had to be stopped. The noise and clamour went on for a full twenty minutes.

Twenty minutes! It was unbelievable. I had made no mistakes, so I think my routine really deserved a 10, but they never gave out 10s in those days. Clearly, the crowd thought it was time to break that unwritten rule.

People were kissing, hugging and congratulating me, and I wasn't sure why. For not falling again? Suddenly, I began to wonder if I was the winner. A 9.85 is an excellent mark. But it wasn't until we mounted the victory stand, and I was shepherded to the second place platform that I finally understood the outcome. Karin Janz was standing above me, in first place, and I was holding a piece of white metal. Second? Why all the congratulations, then? I was waving my hand from force of inertia, but my smile felt stupid and irrelevant. Second.

On to the next apparatus: the beam. Ten thin centimeters of width, but I had to pretend it was 'a huge meadow, and wherever I set my foot would be solid soil'. The illusion seemed foolish, since Latynina and the judges back in the Soviet Union had long ago convinced me that the beam was not my forte. On top of which, Tamara Lazakovich had an 0.05 lead on me after the initial round.

Then, all of a sudden, I felt very calm. I don't know if it was from desolation, or just my goatlike obstinacy taking over. During the warm-up, I did my backward somersault twenty times, flawlessly. I also did as many splits, feeling no tension or fear. I searched the crowd with my eyes and found Ren. He smiled and gave me a thumbs-up sign, which meant: everything is going to be okay, Olga.

Out of curiosity, I watched Tamara's elegant, graceful, feminine routine. She finished her faultless performance and our coaches all hugged and congratulated her. When I saw this, I felt cold rage rising up inside me. I hadn't even gone to the apparatus yet, and they were already congratulating her!

Time to let the obstinate goat get to work. I mounted the beam, and performed my exercise with the precision of a clock. I dismounted in the same perfectly flawless way, and looked over at the judges. 9.90. The gold was mine. Well, okay. That was *much* better.

I sat down on the bench, very relieved, and then noticed Tamara Lazakovich next to me, crying her heart out. What had I done? Grief and despondency came to replace the anger I had felt only a few moments before.

But there was no time for excuses or explanations. The first chords of 'The Mischievous Girl' rang out, and I was already dancing and leaping fiercely, like a bundle of nerves suddenly let loose on the mat. My strength and inspiration left me with the final 'la!' of the music, but they had lasted just long enough. Why had accompanist Evsei Vevrick been so upset when Ren and I changed the music? The 'Mischievous Girl' had turned out to be such a beauty!

I raised my hands happily, sent kisses to the spectators, and went to the bench. The crowd went wild, their thunderous 'Olga! Olga!' thumping inside me along with my heartbeat. During the routine, I had felt as though they all wanted to come out on the mat and help me. It was wonderful to have all of Munich behind me, and I knew that I would now have the pleasure of going to the victory dais to receive another little piece of yellow metal.

For the second time that night, the little girl wearing lucky/unlucky number 253 on her back had won the gold.

Chapter Eight

It is hard to describe what that night was like to anyone who wasn't there. I guess the best description I ever read of the scene was in a book called *Olga*, by an American writer named Justin Beecham. For someone who had no idea what was going on behind the scenes, he conveyed the story with incredible accuracy and insight. I don't know him, but to this day, I thank him for that.

After the victory ceremonies, Tourischeva, Janz, Lazakovich and I had real problems trying to escape from the dense pack of journalists. We had to struggle through the mob, but managed to give away smiles and autographs as we did. Trying to deceive the spectators, the Sportshalle officials took us through an emergency exit, but by the time we were inside our bus, a tremendous crowd had flooded into the entire space around it. I don't know if the bus moved on its own, or was moved by the sea of people. Certainly, if it had not been for the Munich police, we would never have reached our rooms that night.

When I opened the door to my room and turned on the lights, I couldn't believe my eyes. Within a split second, I veered from confusion, to surprise, to delight, to amazement. The room was filled with so many flowers that I could barely step inside. There were bouquets everywhere, and letters and telegrams were spilling from the table and chairs.

I picked up one of the telegrams and read: 'Don't despair, Olga, we are with you!' Another said: 'Olga, your fall is no big deal, just an accident. Forget it!' The telegrams were written in Russian, English, French, German, Japanese. . . .

I climbed over the piles of flowers, and fell on to my bed, utterly exhausted. In my wildest dreams, I never would have imagined such a night.

I was so worn out that I slept for about two days straight. The Games, after all, had been my first major gymnastics event, and now my life felt as though it had been turned completely upside down. Suddenly I had fame and success – plus a bad back.

Ironically, people like Larissa Latynina, who had always criticized me, were now trying to take credit for creating me. Tokarev, a writer for the *Sovietski Sport* who taken every opportunity in the past to denigrate Ren and me, was now writing laudatory articles. Of course, none of the people who were conveniently basking in my reflected glory ever even mentioned Ren, omitting to give him the credit he deserved.

While I slept on endlessly, Ren had been coming to the fence in an attempt to see me. More than once, my team-mates tried to call to me, or shake me awake, but I was too worn out to respond. All of the accumulated tension from the pre-Olympic months of training, and the competition itself, had finally found a relief valve, and I was taking advantage of it.

I woke up that first morning, realizing that everything was over, and I could just let myself relax and do nothing. So I gave myself one more day to enjoy that unthinkable state of bliss which I would not experience again for a long time.

When I finally emerged into the outside world, I found out how famous I had really become. The golden sun, the green trees, the passers-by: everything and everybody seemed to be smiling at me. No matter where I went, people would stop me, say something in a friendly voice, and then ask me to autograph a scratch pad, a postcard, or just a plain sheet of paper. I could not understand what they were saying, since none of them spoke Russian, but I just smiled and gave my autograph to all of them.

Everyone, old and young, knew me. I would go to a shop, looking for presents to bring home to my family, and the shopkeepers would just give me everything free. I never really got to spend any of my money, because I was getting gifts everywhere. I'd be walking through a store, and a line of people would seem to form behind me, offering me hankies, trinkets, anything I wanted.

With the new technology of communications satellites, the Games had been watched all over the world, and the extent of my fame was overwhelming. I would be walking down the street in Munich and the buses would stop so that all the people could get out and ask for my autograph. Passing buses actually stopped! I could hardly go anywhere without being deluged by fans. I was only seventeen, from a poor family in Grodno, and this was all a little too much for me.

Finally, I ended up buying a black wig, a wide-brimmed hat, and a raincoat to wear whenever I was out in public. The disguise helped a little, but even so, people often recognized me.

Walking through the cosy alleys of the Olympic Village, a multilingual crowd would instantly gather about me, and people would give me small pins and other souvenirs, most of which I would just hand to someone else who seemed to want anything that I had touched.

Then, in the canteen, I found the entire Soviet Women's Gymnastics Team having a feast. This temporary lift of our dietary restrictions – always, we had to be thin – was very unusual, and the mounds of food on the table meant we could indulge ourselves to the full. Soon, our lives would go back to normal: we would sweat in the gym, refuse ourselves the food we craved, go to sleep at a regular hour. But, ever so briefly, we had earned the privilege to do whatever we wanted, and we took advantage of it.

Some other athletes moved their table next to ours, followed by another table, and another, until everyone in the mess hall had crowded into our corner of the room, and a celebration in our honour had begun. We were congratulated by athletes from all over the world and although we couldn't understand them, I'm sure they said a lot of nice things to us. They rejoiced with us over our success, and the fact that we had already gone through the competitions that still lay ahead for most of them. Perhaps they wanted to share in our victory, hoping that they could borrow a piece of our luck for their own contests.

Ren had gone back to Grodno by now – his tourist group had had to return – and he was not there to share our joy. How happy he must be, I thought, and what a pity he cannot be here with me now.

I didn't really explore the reasons for his absence; I simply noted it as a fact. Only now do I understand that the leadership of the National Team and Gymnastics Federation were trying to punish him for being ambitious and successful, without ever having attempted to curry their favour. Also, going abroad was not only prestigious, but very profitable. Members of the travelling group were issued 'valuta', a per diem hard currency which could buy things not available in the Soviet Union. People who brought back full suitcases of 'gifts' for the Sports Committee and other decision-makers were generally invited again.

It was fortunate that I was so young then, and unaware of how much filth surrounded me. There were so many ugly political machinations going on. One nasty game of which I was aware, although I didn't fully understand it, concerned the matter of the constant change in my starting number during the competitions. At the pre-Munich training session, I was assigned number two, which meant that I would be the second to perform. The judges have an unwritten rule: the first gymnast gets the lowest score, then it increases for the next gymnast, and so on – unless something unforeseen happens along the way, for example, if someone falls. So, the sixth and final gymnast traditionally gets the highest score. The judges know that the teams are arranged so that the best gymnast goes to the podium last, and that the first one is the weakest.

So, okay, I occupied the second step from the bottom. But on the eve of our departure for Munich, Latynina changed my number to three. 'Raising my price', in a manner of speaking. Once we were in Munich, I was moved up to number four, and then I was placed fifth. Did the senior coach suddenly respect me? No, her interest was purely practical, because she saw a chance to get higher scores for the Soviet team. This, in turn, raised her stock as a trainer. From then on, I often read in our newspapers statements such as: 'The famous Larissa Latynina, who has trained a brilliant assemblage of Soviet gymnasts – Korbut, Tourischeva, Saadi, Lazakovich. . . .' Strange how my name was suddenly at the top of her list.

Why was the simple changing of my number such a negative thing? Think of it this way: try to halt an ordinary pendulum in the middle of its swing. Will it be able to resume its movement at the same rate, with the same rhythm? Not a chance. And the human psyche, especially that of a seventeen-year-old who knew nothing in life other than gymnastics, is a very delicate and sensitive instrument, far more so than a mechanical pendulum.

You see, at the beginning of a meet, you adapt yourself to the situation and get used to every single petty detail: who goes to warm up in front of you, whom you follow to the podium, and so forth. I was being yanked from one place to another, so I never really knew how to prepare. It may sound silly, but most athletes are also rather superstitious, and you don't change a number during the course of a competition any more than a football player would change his shirt during a game. I know that seems trivial, but when you're out there trying to concentrate on competing, it really isn't.

Most people are probably unaware of the degree to which politics used to determine (and sometimes still do determine) the outcome of most major competitions. The International Gymnastics Federation controls everything and, for many years, the Soviet Union has dominated the Federation. Our Socialist system has always heavily influenced the sport.

In an ideal world, the judging would always be honest, but I'm afraid it doesn't work that way. It's better today, since they use six judges, instead of four, but it is still far from perfect. I'm not sure how the judges make their decisions. I really think they just do whatever they want, or whatever they are told. Again, the situation has improved somewhat in recent years.

The spectators have always been my best judges, far better than the real judges, who just sit there and play some kind of game. The audience is always very fair. Ren always said that if the athletes themselves applaud your performance, then you have really achieved your objective. I also figured that if I had enjoyed myself, and loved the routine, then I had done well. I never trusted the judges.

It's hard to believe, but in Munich, they – meaning all of the political powers within the sport – had planned the outcome of each individual event in advance. Lazakovich was to win the beam; Tourischeva, the floor; and the other two events were for the German girls. The Olympics were in Germany, so it was taken for granted that the German athletes would win more than their share of the gymnastics medals. But then I came along and messed everything up by doing so well.

For example, the results in the uneven parallel bars were purely political. I performed a 10, but they gave me a 9.8, so that I would get second place. If I had needed a 9.5 to ensure my getting the silver medal, they would have given me that, instead. In those days, athletes really just played for second place. Obviously, this policy bothered the athletes, but they just accepted it because they had no other choice. Athletes were considered simple cogs in the machine, and easily replaced. It upset me to be a reserve at the World Championships, but complaining about it was really my only option, and even that was strongly discouraged. The National Team leadership made the rules, and we followed them.

It is sad to reflect that during the awards ceremony for the floor exercise, when I won the gold medal, the reason Tourischeva was crying was that she had been told beforehand that *she* would win, so the results were very disappointing. The same was true for Tamara Lasakovich, and the balance beam. I felt guilty about this, because I didn't want them to be hurt, but at the time, I honestly thought that whoever did the best routine would naturally win the event. It was a few years before I found out the unpleasant reality. I deserved to win *three* gold medals in the individual competitions, but I guess, considering what was going on behind closed doors, I was lucky that they gave me any at all.

Everyone who remembers the Munich Olympics knows that there is a serious omission in the events I have just described. The memory most people have of the 1972 Olympics is an unspeakable one, and I haven't even brought it up yet. It must seem utterly callous for me not to have mentioned the terrible tragedy involving the Israeli athletes who were taken hostage and then murdered by their terrorist captors.

The simple truth is that my team-mates and I were never told that this horrible atrocity was happening. We were not actually staying in the Olympic Village at the time, and I knew nothing about it. None of us did. I assume that the rest of the world judged the Soviet athletes to be cold and unfeeling. The truth is we just didn't know. The Sports Committee and our interpreters did not choose to inform us.

I can't remember the exact moment that I found out, but I think it was when I was listening to the radio, after our part in the Games had ended. I couldn't really understand the German announcer, but I heard something about an explosion in Munich, in the Israeli sportsmen's residence, which had taken the lives of many people. I tried to understand the German words, listening in shock and horror.

Why had we not been told?

I went to Larissa Latynina to ask her what had happened. 'Is it true that several Israeli athletes were killed?'

'It's none of our business, Olga,' was all she said.

Then it must be true. The information was staggering, and I felt as though I was speaking from deep·inside a head stuffed with cotton.

'Why didn't they *tell* us?' I asked. 'Why did they conceal it from us?'

'It is none of our business,' Latynina said, again.

I went back to my room, bewildered, and looked at my medals, the medals I had won on top of the graves of my fellow athletes. How horrible! Was it really possible for such a thing to happen? We had all come to Munich to unite the planet in the peaceful harmony of the Olympic Games, and some Arab extremist group had done this vicious, unimaginable thing.

I sat there in a daze. I had so many questions, and there were no answers.

First, was it moral to go on with the Olympics after what had happened? Even now, I find it hard to answer that question with anything like certainty.

Secondly, was it humane to keep all of the Soviet athletes in such a complete informational vacuum? We were segregated whenever we went abroad, and the Sports Committee always did everything in its power to keep us insulated from the outside world. We were only to know what they wanted us to know.

I don't think the leaders of our delegation kept the news of the tragedy a secret from us *only* because of anti-Semitic tendency although that was probably a factor. A more likely explanation is that they didn't want to upset us because stress like that could reduce the flow of gold medals.

How horrible. Was it really worth it to 'spare us' like that? How do 'jangled nerves' and 'sickened stomachs' compare with murder, and death? In any event, the Soviet authorities certainly got the desired results: we were devastated by what had happened, but by then, we had already won. Our victory might be stained with the blood of innocent athletes, but the only thing that mattered to our leaders was that we had come out on top.

I still don't know exactly how to feel about the horror that took place in the Olympic Village that year, and the added obscenity of our being oblivious to it.

Chapter Nine

I felt very homesick now, and wanted to return to Grodno and be with my family. It was time to be *away* from the Olympics, with all of its stresses and notoriety. I wanted to go back to Ren, and my tiny gymnasium, which was so small that I had to pretend I had already taken the first step of my run when I was vaulting. I wanted to get away from Germany, and back to my work.

At the last minute, however, our plans were changed for us. The entire gymnastics team was summoned to a meeting with the National Team leaders, and the leaders of the Sports Committee of the USSR. As I mentioned, we were always surrounded by countless unnecessary officials, who only came along in order to travel and shop. Among ourselves, the athletes called these parasites 'vacuum cleaners'.

The Chairman of the Sports Committee congratulated us again, and then told us his news.

'My dear girls!' he said. 'You have been given the great honour to represent the Soviet gymnastics in the Federal Republic of Germany. Your tour starts tomorrow.'

The room was a silent as a graveyard.

'I appreciate that it is not easy to start up all over again,' he said, 'but it is necessary.'

My least favourite Russian word, 'nado'. Necessary. I had lived my entire life under its burden. The real message behind the official's florid rhetoric was: 'The Soviet Sports Committee needs foreign currency, and it's your responsibility to earn it, girls.'

So, after we had already done our best at the Olympics, expending our entire physical and emotional strength, we had to travel from one city to another for the next two weeks, sometimes performing as often as twice a day. We would have to use non-standard small apparatuses in small school gymnasiums, but that was the least of our problems. It was as though someone had gone up to Bob Beamon, the Olympic long-jump champion at Mexico City in 1968, right after he had jumped an incredible 29 ft $2\frac{1}{2}$ in, and said, 'Good job, Bob, you've done well. Now you have to jump *again*, for at least thirty feet this time.'

The Sports Committee's only interest was making more money, even if it was at the expense of our health and emotional well-being. We were like slave labour to them.

We performed mechanically, squeezing out what little strength was left in our muscles. We did not include very many interesting and unusual elements in these performances because we just didn't have the energy. At the Olympics, I had tried to create pieces of art, but now, we just worked like robots.

I was grateful that our audience forgave us for not being able to show them more. They wanted to see *us* more than they wanted to see our performances. I felt awkward around my team-mates because the public would roar with delight when they saw Olga Korbut, as compared to just seeing members of the USSR National Team. I felt as though I had come out to the centre of a square, completely naked, and all those present were scrutinizing me.

I realized now how right Ren had been to make me get up on the apparatus over and over again, and repeat each movement twenty times, flawlessly.

'If you persuade yourself, my dear,' he would say, 'you will go all over the world. The whole world will worship you, and you will be applauded in all the finest arenas. Because you are what you are, and you represent the gymnastics of tomorrow.'

At the time, I thought that he was deceiving me, trying to manipulate me into going on. I never asked myself why he would do that; I just got angry. But he was right. Everything had happened just the way he said it would.

The strange thing is how quickly it all became boring.

I got tired of not being able to go anywhere without being pestered, and my black wig, hat and raincoat came in very handy. I would only climb out of that shell on the rare occasions when I wanted to savour my popularity again.

During that tour of Germany, the lumbago in my back began to hurt more and more. The novocaine injections took away the pain for a while, but I needed time to rest and heal. By the end of the tour, I walked as though I had a stake in my spine. I was so tired that my temper grew very short, and small things I would ordinarily ignore irritated me intensely.

Sending us on that exhausting tour right after the Olympics was cruel – and potentially dangerous. Athletes are much more likely to injure themselves when they are tired. We all felt dull, hopeless and disoriented. Today, I would not find it unusual to feel that way during such a strenuous tour, but we were all very upset by this lassitude.

Nothing was going right, and none of us could perform well. Tourischeva, Lazakovich, Saadi, Koshel, Burda – none of us. Only a few days before, we had been winning medals, but now our muscles felt stiff and leaden. We were all still practically children, and no one told us that we needed time to calm down mentally, as well as physically. I just felt helpless and battered.

If not for that tour, who knows? Maybe I wouldn't have developed the hopeless apathy which controlled my life for the next few years. As far as the Sports Committee was concerned, it didn't matter if we were traumatized by going on intensive, money-making tours. Everyone in my country was considered equal, so if they lost these gymnasts, others would come to take their places.

Finally, the tour was over, and we flew into the Sheremetevo Airport in Moscow. They made us stay for a long official welcome ceremony, even though we were sick and tired of all the pomp and circumstance. I just wanted to find a sofa, and sleep forever.

I thought the train ride from Moscow to Grodno would never end. It seemed as though I would be spending the rest of my life on that train. When it stopped, after what seemed to be centuries, some young men came pushing into my compartment.

'Are you Olga Korbut?' they asked.

I nodded, and they took me to a truck, with a special platform built on the back. I rode on that platform through the entire city. I think I was feeling happy, and smiled, but maybe I didn't. My strongest memories of that entire period are fatigue, pain, and the empty feeling of being a fly whose blood has been sucked out by a predatory spider.

The 1972 Olympics were both the best, and the worst, time of my life.

In Germany, I had been a star. In the Soviet Union, it was quite a different story. Especially in Grodno. People would call my parents, and say ironically, 'So I see your daughter is getting, what, famous?' Once, someone even threw garbage at our front door. I don't know, I suppose it was envy. That, or stupidity. People knew how poor we had always been and now, suddenly, I was a success. In my country, because everyone is supposed to be equal, success is not considered a good thing. That is why so many of our most talented people have left the Soviet Union to go to America and other countries. The Party Leadership would do everything possible to encourage anyone with a sense of individuality to leave. I can't understand the psychology behind that; you would think they would want to hang on to their most talented citizens and take credit for their achievements. I suppose it was just that same old Stalinist mentality. Everyone is replaceable; no one is special. I probably should have expected people to resent me, but it really came as a surprise.

While I was still in Munich, one of my many telegrams had been from the Grodno State University. It read: 'Congratulations on your admission to the Faculty of History at our University!' Well, okay. Perhaps they wished me well. On the other hand, maybe they just wanted to have an Olympic champion as a member of their student body. The thought of what people would say behind my back terrified me.

'You know, they've taken her in without admission exams,' I could imagine people whispering when I passed by. 'You think she's going to study like you and me? No way. Next time she shows up here will be in five years when it's time to collect her diploma.'

I did not want those whispers to be true, so when I got home, I sat down with all of the textbooks and began to read. The University made an exception for me, and allowed me to take exams later than everyone else.

Imagine a schoolgirl who, since the fourth grade, had practically stopped going to school. By the seventh grade, the teachers had forgotten my name. And yet, somehow, I continued to receive marks for my 'studies'.

'You don't have time for both school and sports,' Ren always said to me. 'To me, quite frankly, your studies are immaterial.'

Since that was what my Lord and Master thought, I never doubted that he was right, and I stopped thinking about school. So you can imagine the incredible mountain of text-books I now had to read.

I can't say that I was able to master every one of those subjects in the next several weeks, but I learned a lot, and considered myself fully prepared to face the most difficult exams. And if I failed, I hoped that the professors would feel at least a small amount of sympathy for me. After all, I was an Olympic champion, and the pride of Grodno, right?

How wrong I was. When the professor of history, a skinny old man, entered the room, I naïvely took him for a kind-hearted grandfather. But his very first remarks proved me wrong.

'I only know ancient Greek Olympic champions,' he declared. 'If you hope your medals are an asset, we can say goodbye to each other right here and now.'

I was not about to admit that I entertained such hopes. But inwardly, I bristled, and prepared myself for a major battle.

The professor interrogated me at length, visibly enjoying himself as he waited for the moment when I would open my mouth helplessly and have nothing to say. However, I rose to the challenge, wriggling like a snake in a frying pan, evading his traps, and using all of my cunning to evade unfamiliar questions. Eventually he was forced to surrender.

'Although your knowledge of the subject is not crystal clear,' he said, finally, 'in general, I must admit that you have an understanding of the essence of historical processes and their interconnection.'

I like to think that maybe, for the first time in his life, he thought warmly about sports, and their power to provide a person with an unlimited reserve of moral and physical strength with which to fight life's hardships.

So, they accepted me as a student – not because of my medals, but because of the four Bs I had earned at the entry exams. I was able to put an end to all of the gossip before it even started.

In the years that followed, I wasn't exactly an ideal student. I spent twelve to fourteen hours in the gym every day, and nearly half of the year on the road. The only way I could study was if I packed my textbooks into my suitcases and read them at night in the strange, distant cities where I was training or competing. I was allowed to work on independent study, instead of attending classes, and my instructors' only concern was that I be prepared for all exams.

But all that came later. In the meantime, I was living a new and unusual post-Olympics life. After Munich, I got so many letters that I could not even read all of them. They had to assign a special clerk at the post office just to sort out my personal mail. At that point, I was getting as many as twenty thousand letters a year.

At first, with my mother and sisters' help, I tried to answer all of them. When the burden got too heavy for us, some students from the University and Grodno College pitched in, yet still we could not keep up with the pace. We decided then that we would answer people who had already written twice, and anyone who had enclosed an envelope with their return address. Even then, it was time-consuming work, and we were always way behind. Once, I actually found a gold coin inside a letter that had been sent two or three years earlier.

I had to use a lot of ingenuity to evade the brash journalists who would come into our home as though it belonged to them, and start asking the same questions I had answered hundreds of times before. I also had to speak to groups of students, teachers and workers, telling them (for the one-thousandth time) about the Olympiad.

Although I was too young to possess a driver's licence, I had a car. I would drive it around, and the Grodno police would always look the other way. When I was finally old enough under Soviet law, they simply fished me out, took me to a police station and handed my new licence to me.

The day after I finally got my licence, I was on my way to a meeting at one of the colleges when I was involved in a terrible car accident. The light was green and I was going through an intersection when I saw a bus turning from a side street straight into my path. I was going pretty fast and would never have been able to stop in time, but gymnastics and the memory of trained muscles came to my rescue. Of their own will, my legs pushed me over the front seat and into the back. At least, I think that's what happened – all I know for sure is that I found myself in the back seat. Just as well. The steering wheel had smashed right through the back of the driver's seat.

I couldn't believe that I had survived the terrible crash, and I jumped out of the car to yell at the drunken bus driver. Then, trembling all over, I hurried to the nearby college to attend my meeting.

After the meeting (incredibly I sat right through it) I started to realize what a close call I had had. My mother turned up in a frantic state. Some 'kind' neighbours had heard about the crash, and told her that I was dead.

'Your Olga got into an accident and was killed,' they said. 'Somebody saw her head rolling on the asphalt.'

When my mother saw me, she felt me all over to make sure I was alive and well. When she found only a small bleeding scratch on my head, she collapsed on the sidewalk and started crying.

Ren, who must have heard the same story about my un-
timely death, also showed up. Once he, too, was sure that
I was intact, he started yelling at me.

'Fool!' he said furiously. 'You could have killed yourself!'

That must have been the last straw because after repressing
the urge to slug him, I sank down on to the sidewalk next
to my mother and started crying with her.

The funny part is that after a delegation of that bus driver's
relatives came to me, pleading for clemency, I went to the
police station myself and asked them not to punish the man.
I even begged them to restore his licence.

All that aside, with the Olympics over, my life was slowly
but surely beginning to return to normal. The excitement
was gone, and the doctors had managed to improve, if not
cure, my lumbago. I spent lots of time at the Red Banner
School Gym because no unauthorized people were allowed
inside and that way, I was able to hide from my fans.

I was still working with Ren, but he was not training me
in the same intense way as before. One day, looking pens-
ive, he motioned for me to sit down.

'I need to talk to you,' he said.

Sensing some strange change in his voice and expression
and wondering what it meant, I obediently sat down.

'Olga,' he said, and then sighed. 'Maybe enough is
enough!'

I looked at him blankly. 'What is enough?'

He sighed again. 'Gymnastics.'

What? Now, I stared at him.

'It was a long honest road to Munich, and we have come
to the end of it,' he said. 'You didn't win the all-around, but
that's not important. The main thing is that you've seen the
world. People watched you, and loved you. You demonstrated the gymnastics they have never seen, and will not
see again in the near future.'

I had never known him to act like this before. My cool,
even-tempered Ren, who let emotions show on his face
once every twenty years, was agitated and uneasy as a boy
on his first date.

'You're a star now, but you've reached your limit,' he said. 'You won't do more than you've already done.'

I started to protest, but he stopped me by raising his hand.

'No, you haven't made use of even half your potential,' he agreed. 'You have not achieved all you could have. But you won't be able to. You've spent yourself. That's okay because we have proved to everyone that our gymnastics is the way of the future. So, leave the sport. Leave it now, and with grace. You've sparkled – that's enough.'

I sat there, unable to comprehend what I was hearing.

'The world will remember you the way you were in Munich,' Ren said. 'Your subsequent performances will look faded by comparison, and each time you go out on the podium, you'll be breaking off a small piece of the image of you that people have built in their minds.'

I was speechless. Leave gymnastics, now? When everything was so wonderful? When my whole life, so beautiful and promising, was still ahead of me? Impossible! But Ren was looking at me, waiting for my response, and I had to say something.

'And what will happen to me if I do?' I asked. 'How will I live?'

'We shall go away,' he said.

What? 'Where?' I asked. 'What for?'

'We'll go to the Caucasus, to the sea,' he promised. 'We'll buy a house and live together.'

Could this really be my beloved teacher telling me these things? I swallowed. 'You want me to marry you?'

He shook his head. 'We'll live together . . .'

I couldn't listen any more. Ren kept talking, trying to convince me, but I didn't hear him. Disjointed snatches of his phrases would get through, as if they were coming from a faraway tunnel, but I just sat there. I felt as if I should get up and leave, or *say* something, but I couldn't make myself move or speak.

Ren, my mythological Zeus who belonged somewhere up there on high where gods ride their golden chariots, had descended to me and offered – no! A permanent crack had now been forged in our relationship, threatening my ability to work, all because he hadn't managed to maintain the distance that should always exist between a teacher and his pupil. The Emperor had come down from his throne, and now my trust and respect were gone for good.

For the first time in my life, I realized that the only person I could rely on was myself.

Chapter Ten

I don't know why Ren decided to talk to me in that way. Maybe he thought that, under the circumstances, I simply would not be able to prepare myself properly for the next Olympics. I had my college studies, all those meetings, and a chain of demonstration tours in foreign states. Could there be any serious training when I had that many conflicts of interest? Besides, he had already achieved the results he wanted. Whatever his reasons, I don't think that it was the sort of conversation he should have had at that particular time with such a trusting teenager.

Looking back, I think that he could not, or possibly did not, even try to see me as a human being – live person, with shortcomings and occasional whims. That would explain not only that conversation, but many other events in my gymnastics life with him. He had not even tried to understand what was going on in my soul, what impact any careless words would have on a young girl who had just started to mature. He really thought of me as merely some suitable material for his experiments. As his property.

Why had he suggested that I leave, when I had only just begun my career? Munich, after all, was my first major competition. I guess it was because he had managed to prove to the world, to Latynina, to the Sports Committee, that his brand of gymnastics not only had a right to exist, but represented the future of the sport. We have proved it, he said, but that was wrong. I wasn't trying to prove anything. I was just doing the thing I loved best.

Many years later, in an article published in *Pravda*, Ren told the journalist a lot of things which may explain his suggestion that I leave sports. He said that he had never really wanted to be a coach, and that he thought of Elena Voltchetskaya as the only real pupil he had ever had. He said that with me, he just built upon what he had already established with her, hoping to find acceptance from the powers that be. That I, Olga Korbut, was almost beside the point.

I don't know if he was being sincere then, or back in 1972, when he spoke so intensely to me. Even now, I really can't understand what kind of person he is, despite all the time I spent with him. He was, for me, both a father and a demon. He had a very strong, even abusive, personality. He wanted to make me what *he* wanted me to be, forgetting that I was a person who might have some ideas of her own. It was only during competitions, when he couldn't prevent me, that I could do as I pleased. I think he looked at me as a machine. I was just getting started in gymnastics when he told me that I had to quit. It was a crucial time in my life, and I think he abandoned me.

He used to say to me, 'Oh, you'll see, I'll make a lot of girls just like you. I will coach them, and make them great.' But really, I was the only one.

I wish I had known as much then as I do now. Would that have changed anything? Would I have listened to him, and given up gymnastics at the peak of my fame? Would I have done that, and taken the path to nowhere? On the contrary, I think I would have been strong enough to break off my relationship with him right then to continue my work with someone else. It would have saved both of us a lot of pain.

Ren's second suggestion – or, rather, proposition – was even more disturbing. Did he really want me to become his wife, or just serve in the dubious position of a kept woman for a year or so? I often ask myself if it is possible that I was in love with him, in my own childish way. I don't think so. I respected him, of course, and I was afraid of him, but love? No. For me, he was Coach, Lord and Master, Devil, Judge and Hangman. What he wanted to become – a lover – was the last thing I wanted.

Was he in love with me? Probably, yes. But it was a very narcissistic sort of love, since he loved not me, but himself *in* me. He considered me his creation, and that was probably accurate. But, at some point, the genie escaped from the bottle, and once we had that conversation in the gym that day, there was no way to drive the genie back inside again.

I now found myself in a terrible state of depression. Prostration, really. The shock of my coach's betrayal coming after all of the stresses of the Olympics, was a blow from which I could not seem to recover.

Ren did not react to this in any way. He had suggested; I had refused; and that was that. At least, it seemed that way on the surface. We resumed our work-outs as though nothing had happened. The smell of chalk, foam rubber mats, the explosive sounds of the beatboard and his constant echoing commands, were the only medicine I knew.

Nevertheless, my attitude had definitely changed. I no longer flew to the gym, or even walked briskly. I had to drag myself every step of the way, saying over and over, 'It is necessary, Olga, it's necessary.'

Ren must have been aware of this because he didn't push me to work harder, but just talked to me quietly. He could sense my fear and desperation when I approached each apparatus, and he would clap his hands earlier than usual, saying, 'Okay, that's it for the day.'

That clap always sounded like the lock snapping on my prison cell door.

What had happened to me? Was that sensation of freedom and joy still hidden in some secret corner of my soul? I was trying to find it in myself, and glue all of the little pieces back together, but somehow, I couldn't.

Maybe it really *was* time to quit. Maybe Ren was right. I had achieved everything I could have wanted. I was only eighteen, and I had won three Olympic gold medals and a silver. I was a student at a prestigious college, and I had my whole future ahead of me. But what *was* that future? What could I do other than gymnastics? Maybe I should just dump everything, get married, have a bunch of kids, and try to get my diploma. I didn't know *what* to do. I kept trying to drive all of those contradictory thoughts away, but they always came back. I was in a complete panic, and hated myself for it.

Later on, a journalist who was trying to explain my condition at that time brought me a psychology book and showed me the section on what psychologists call 'the achievement disease'. Essentially, it said that if you reached all of your goals, the enormity of the achievement was almost impossible to handle. The inevitable results were panic and depression.

Sounds like an accurate diagnosis to me.

Yet no matter how hard and painful the process was, Ren and I still tried to move forward. Once more, he began to give me new elements to learn, his uncontrollable fantasies pushing him on. Having reconciled himself to the fact that his obstinate pupil would not give in and quit, he was now preparing me for the World Championships, which were to be held in Varna in 1974.

The measured rhythm of our training was suddenly interrupted by the spectre of Larissa Latynina, who appeared in our gymnasium one day in 1973.

'Pack your travel bags, folks!' she said cheerfully. 'The plane to the United States of America leaves tomorrow.'

Ren and I looked at each other.

'But –' he started.

'No 'buts' accepted,' Latynina said, pretending to be hearty. 'They have invited the National Team, but on one condition: that Korbut be on the list. So, don't waste time, pack your suitcases. We're leaving for Moscow today.'

So, how about that? The senior coach of the National Team had come personally to invite a gymnast whom she did not even consider as one of the team leaders. It was very hard for me to understand the motivations and intrigues of the Moscow authorities, although it was perfectly in keeping with what had happened when the team had been ordered to take another tour of West Germany. As usual, Ren was not invited to come along, and I decided to refuse, too.

'I won't go,' I told Latynina.

Her smile was jovial, and pitiless. 'You will, my dear. You have no alternatives.'

I ended up hiding in a rest room at the Sheremetevo Airport, crying in a stall. No one could find me, and the leaders of the National Team were in a complete uproar. Several times, I heard Latynina's voice come over the PA system, demanding that I return to the team immediately. I didn't, and the plane took off without me.

A day later, the team was back in Moscow, everybody angry and offended. The Germans had refused to receive the team, saying, 'We are sorry, dear ladies, but we invited Korbut. . .'

Fabergé, the company that had organized the twenty-day tour of the United States, had laid down the same condition. So Larissa Latynina had to come in person to Grodno to fetch a very stubborn young gymnast. In those days, I wasn't even aware that every single exhibition tour contract the National Team received had a separate line in it, stipulating my mandatory participation.

Although Ren and Latynina argued at length, we ended up going to America. It was the first of my five or six tours around the United States, and I remember every single fantastic moment of it.

When we arrived at JFK, a friendly hostess opened the massive hatch to let us out one by one. The crowd outside was so large that it looked like a human ocean. Large posters read: 'Welcome, Olga!' 'Olga!' and 'Korbut and Soviet Team in US for the First Time!' I was surprised by the extent of my popularity, and felt uncomfortable in front of my team-mates, especially Tourischeva. It was she who had been the All-Around champion of the Munich Olympic Games, not me! I couldn't help wondering if they were honouring me by mistake, but that was definitely my name on all those posters. What a great welcome!

My first impression of America was that everything was so *big*! Enormous limousines, tremendous skyscrapers, and, of course, my huge bodyguard, Bill. I also remember the wave of emotion sweeping over a country that had never exactly been regarded as a paradise for gymnasts. After the Munich

Olympics, however, gymnastics had become so popular in the States that many other sports were being pushed aside. Previously, it would have been hard to imagine a male American who did not play baseball; now it seemed equally hard to imagine that his daughter was not studying gymnastics. In post-Munich America, Olga Korbut gymnastics classes and clubs seemed to be springing up like mushrooms after a spring rain.

Not too long ago, I came across an old newspaper clipping, yellowed with age, the article describing our first tour of the United States. It talked about me being greeted at the Los Angeles Airport by a crowd of young people wearing 'Olga Korbut Fan Club' T-shirts and sweatshirts. 'I anticipated a warm welcome,' I was quoted as saying, 'but not *that* warm!' And everywhere I went, I got that same kind of wonderful reception.

Discarding false modesty, I have to admit that I probably had something to do with making gymnastics so unprecedentedly popular in the United States.

I seemed to hear my name not daily or hourly, but almost every minute: on the radio, on television programmes, and then splashed all over the newspapers and magazines. I kept seeing pictures of my weeping face after my fall in Munich, next to pictures of my jubilant smile after winning the gold medals. Somehow, gymnastics in America was invariably linked to my name, and there were dozens of different versions of 'Cinderella' stories written about the little girl from Grodno. The little girl was me, and the plot always revolved around my fall and my tears at Munich.

We had a great time in America, especially in comparison with other tours where we had to perform twice a day. This time, we only had to do one two-hour programme every three days. It was like being on vacation.

However, the two-hour programme presented a problem. Each of our performances took, at most, ninety seconds, and there were only six of us: Ludmilla Tourischeva, Tamara Lazakovich, Luba Bogdanova, Tonya Koshel, Rusudan Sikharulidze, and me. Multiply six by ninety seconds, and you only get nine minutes. How were we going to fill the other one hundred and eleven minutes? Finally, we decided to include our warm-ups in the programme – let Americans enter 'the kitchen' of our gymnastics – and save our performances for the end.

It occurred to me that the composition of our team was different from the group that went to Munich, even though it had been advertised as the Olympic squad. What had happened to Elvira Saadi and Luboc Burda? The explanation is disgustingly banal – Burda and Saadi's coaches were not skilled in flattering Latynina and the other heads of Soviet gymnastics. Luba Bogdanova, on the other hand, was from prosperous Moscow, and Sikharulidze was from the very rich province of Georgia. I am not casting aspersions on their gymnastic abilities, but certainly *their* coaches commanded influence. If Fabergé, the company underwriting the tour, had not insisted upon my participation, I know that I would not have been invited either.

Further evidence, I suppose, of the corruption permeating Soviet gymnastics.

The tour was beautifully organized. The schedule was so undemanding that I actually enjoyed performing again. When I ran to the apparatus on the podium, I no longer felt the weight of my recent depression. During my routines, I would forget about everything else, and simply improvise, trying to please both myself and the public who had come to watch me. I'm sure the Soviet Union took a good percentage of the profits – considering how many tickets were sold – but that was the only tour on which we were not used as money-making machines. On most of the others, our bodies were punished beyond reason just so that our government could get more dollars, pounds, francs or marks.

As I have mentioned, my family back home desperately needed everyday things like shoes and clothing. To save money, my team-mates and I developed a clever trick. Taking into account the fact that nearly all of us were dieting, the meals provided for each girl were enough for three or four of us. So we asked the tour organizers to give us the cash equivalent, instead of the actual food. It probably didn't seem a lot to them, but to us, those pennies were a fortune. On subsequent trips, we even brought soup concentrates, canned food and salami from home, so that we didn't have to spend a single cent of hard currency on ourselves. That way, we could buy much-needed supplies for our families in the Soviet Union.

The leaders of our group were perfectly aware of our fiddles with the currency, but they warned us never to mention that we did not have enough money when we returned to Moscow. After all, the funds were in their hands and we received only what they chose to give us. It seems clear that more than a little graft was taking place.

In the United States, we were pleasantly surprised to find normal, standard apparatuses and huge arenas everywhere we went, compared with the small school gymnasiums where we had performed in West Germany. In America, we appeared at places like Madison Square Garden, with an average capacity of fifteen to seventeen thousand spectators. Astonishingly, even with such big facilities, we always sold out.

As soon we came out to the podium, those huge halls would erupt with applause, foot stamping and cheering. Both in warm-up and actual performance, explosion of enthusiasm would greet every tiniest detail of our routines, whether an unexpected or risky transfer, a graceful gesture or a simple wave of the hand. So you can imagine the response I would get for my trademark back flip on the beam, or for a loop on the bars. Our American audiences were just terrific.

I was now soaring as though I had grown wings. My smile would appear automatically when I looked into the eyes of those sincere, loving and expectant crowds. I forgot about my fatigue. The feeling of absolute contact with the audiences can only be compared with what I had felt in Munich. In the light of my recent problems, though, this feeling was even more precious.

We took immense pleasure in listening to what translators read to us from the local newspapers, and in seeing our happy faces on television – and we always had a pen handy for autographs!

The phenomenal boom in American gymnastics started in 1972, and was further boosted by our National Team exhibitions. At that point, there really weren't any top-notch American gymnasts, so students of the sport watched our warm-ups as eagerly as they watched the performances, trying to learn as much as they could. They must have learned quickly because within two or three years, we were already seeing new and interesting American athletes at the big international meets. They did not yet pose a threat in all-round competitions, but in some of the individual events, their routines were causing a real furore. Unaccustomed to having serious competition from that part of the world, we would look across the ocean in amazement. Today, American gymnasts have joined the ranks of those who determine the future course of world gymnastics.

On that first tour in 1973, we performed alone, but the next year – and ever since – American gymnasts participated in our exhibitions, and we enjoyed having them.

During that tour, I felt better than I had for a long time, but my depression still hadn't vanished completely. Sometimes I had that exhilarating sensation of soaring, but at other times, I thought I could actually hear my tired joints cracking apart. I didn't want to disappoint anyone, and I would have been ashamed not to show people what they had been expecting to see. But I was very, very tired.

The audiences were kind, seeming not to notice my slips and flaws, and praising each microscopic success as though it were a gigantic victory. I was extremely grateful for that.

Also, I have to admit, I was glad that Ren had come on the tour with us. If he hadn't been there, I think I would have spent a lot of time hiding away in my room, crying into my pillow because I felt so weak and tired. I think he, too, must have heard the cracking sounds in my joints and bones, because he never scolded me or insisted that I correct my mistakes. Like the American public, he turned a blind eye to my flaws. At the same time, when I actually did something well, he was full of praise.

'That's my girl!' he would say. 'Well done!'

I knew that the one thing I couldn't do was fall during any of my performances. I was determined not to disillusion anyone. Nor did I want the hypocritical sympathy from Latynina and the others. The last thing I craved was anyone's pity. I kept my doubts and despair deep inside, and am pretty sure that none of them noticed what a hard time I was having.

Unfortunately, the Olga Korbut who came to the United States was a very poor replica of the Korbut who had dazzled the world in Munich the year before.

Chapter Eleven

In the middle of the American tour, we went to Washington, DC. On the first day, our morning training session was cancelled for some reason. I was very upset because I felt I needed every second of that practice time.

'At 11.00,' our leader announced, 'our delegation will be received by Richard Nixon.'

'What's going on?' I asked Ren grumpily. 'Couldn't that Nixon fellow come for an autograph himself? I need to train!'

Ren laughed. 'Richard Nixon isn't an autograph seeker, Olga. He doesn't give a damn about your signature. He's the President of this country – the biggest shot here. He just wants to meet you, and have a chat.'

I was somewhat appeased, though angry at our practice being cancelled so unceremoniously. I was still the little girl who had been snatched out of the fourth grade and whose knowledge of the world around me extended only to the local gymnasiums and hotels. In all honesty, I didn't really know who Nixon was. The only literature I had ever read were textbooks focusing, for the most part, on the Soviet Union and the Communist Party, and those parts of newspapers that reported our exhibitions. My real education only began after I quit gymnastics for good.

When it was explained to me that the President ordinarily did not receive sports delegations, and our visit to the White House was an extraordinarily important and solemn event, I started to get nervous.

A large crowd of reporters was waiting for us. We were taken inside and given a twenty-minute tour of the Chief

Executive's mansion. I listened to the presentation being given by the friendly guides, and tapped my foot impatiently. When would he come, this Nixon, the number-one man in America? I could not understand why he should invite us, and then not bother to show up.

Suddenly, a tall, wide-shouldered and smiling man cut through the crowd of reporters. Was this the President? He looked like a nice enough guy. He came over to me, and I had to tilt my head up to look at him.

'Wow, what a little girl you are!' he said.

I forgot that I was not at home in Grodno, swapping insults with a boy from the next block, and my mouth opened before I could stop myself.

'Wow, what a big boy *you* are!' I replied perfectly mimicking his intonations.

My tongue has always been my enemy. How could I have said such a thing to the President of the United States? I was trying to think of a polite way out of the situation when all the Americans, including the 'big boy', burst into laughter. I was greatly relieved, and started laughing myself, pretending that the remark was one I had carefully planned and not simply a foolish blunder.

President Nixon shook hands with everyone, saying nice things to each one of us, and demonstrating a remarkable knowledge of our backgrounds as he greeted us. He presented the girls with White House brooches, and the men with similar pairs of cufflinks. Noticing that the cufflinks were smaller than the brooches, I couldn't help casting a gloating glance at Ren.

His return glance, unnoticed by the others, said: What a dear little fool you are, Olga.

The presentation ceremony had none of the formality or fuss to which we were accustomed. We were simply told that the brooches were our gifts, each girl was given one, and that was that. There was no pomp or flourish, which were absolute requirements in Russia. In fact, our entire visit to the White House was very pleasant and unpretentious.

Before we left, Richard Nixon spoke to us briefly, without any prepared notes. A Russian official would have yanked a lengthy text from his pocket and recited the entire thing.

'You are gymnasts,' the President said. 'You jump and roll, and fly headlong over the apparatus – and you always land on your feet. I think we politicians have a lot to learn from you. In particular, this skill – always handy in any extreme situation – of landing firmly on your feet. In our troubled times, that is a most valuable quality.'

Now I was *really* glad I had gone through the entire tour so far without a single fall. If I had fallen, I would not only have let down myself, and Ren, and the audience, but also the President of the United States.

After eighteen days, our tour approached its end. I was packing my suitcases with numerous gifts for my family, and looking forward to a few days of rest, when Ren came into my room with a big smile on his face.

'Olga, do you remember you called me a shameless liar when I said that you would go all over the world, and people would worship you?' he asked.

I remembered it very well.

'Well, guess what?' he said.

Apparently a cable had been sent from the United States to the USSR. It was addressed to Alexey N. Kosygin, at the Kremlin in Moscow, and it was from Mayor Richard Daley of Chicago, inviting the Soviet National Women's Gymnastics Team – me, in particular – to Chicago, a city we had missed on our tour.

Travelling around the world is very nice when it is only in your dreams. Once I embarked on it, however I always longed to go home.

When I learned that our authorities had immediately accepted this kind invitation, I was close to tears. I wanted to be on a plane to *Moscow*, not Chicago.

My despair evaporated when we landed at O'Hare airport and were greeted by a gigantic, cheering crowd. All the newspapers had banner headlines, trumpeting our arrival, and no matter where I looked, I saw happy and loving admirers. It was impossible for me to be sad.

We had always thought of Chicago as the capital of American gangsters. It was Al Capone's favourite place. Instead, here was a city that seemed to worship gymnastics, and *adored* me. It was a perfect final stop for our tour. We performed, as always, to full houses, the audiences demanding many encores. We had such a good time that I was no longer mad at Richard Daley. At a reception in our honour, he rose at the end, and gave a speech that thrilled me.

'From now on and until the end of time,' he proclaimed, 'March 26 is declared "Olga Korbut Day" in Chicago, and she herself is now declared an Honorary Citizen of Chicago.'

Each year, until the early eighties, the postman in Grodno, and later Minsk, would punctually deliver me an invitation to visit Chicago. 'Dear Miss Korbut, You are cordially invited to participate. . .' When the invitations finally stopped coming, I worried that I might have offended Mayor Daley and the citizens of his wonderful city. How could I explain to them that I lived in a country separated from the rest of the world by an impenetrable iron curtain, in which there existed a unique concept: 'Nevyezdnoi'. That means 'Unreliable, not subject to travel abroad.' I would have liked nothing better than to respond to those invitations. When I finally *did* make it back to the United States, I was very sad to learn that Mayor Daley had died.

There were two other important incidents I remember on my initial visit to Chicago.

On one occasion our bus stopped on a quiet street, away from the crowds. We had been hoping to take a walk on the streets of the city without being recognized, but were soon surrounded by autograph collectors. For an hour, we signed everything the fans gave us, and it probably would have gone on forever if we hadn't been able to sneak back on to our bus, one by one. When the door finally closed behind us, we sighed in relief.

I was sitting surrounded by the other girls, because if people recognized me, the bus would have to stop again and the whole chaotic scene would be repeated. I happened to look back, and saw a boy – maybe twelve years old –

who was walking on his hands after the bus. The bus had accelerated, and the distance between us was increasing, but he kept doggedly following us. Ten meters, thirty, fifty, one hundred. . .

'Stop, please!' I yelled to the driver, the rest of the team joining in.

When the driver looked in his rear view mirror and saw the boy, he slowed down. Then, he stopped the bus and we all got out.

The boy rolled forward, stood up, and offered me a sheet of paper.

'Miss Korbut, your autograph, please,' he said.

Naturally, we all signed his paper. Who could refuse?

The other incident was much more serious. Someone had called the local police to say, 'There are plans to assassinate Olga Korbut. She may not leave Chicago alive.' Then the caller, either a well-wisher who was afraid to identify himself or a vicious scoundrel, hung up.

'Baloney,' said my new American friends, trying to allay my fears. 'That can't be serious. They are only trying to upset you.'

I have to admit that it is very unpleasant to live with the thought that at any moment you might hear a shot – from a passing car, from under your bed, or from a twenty-fifth-floor window of the skyscraper across the street. Every sound made me jump, and I wanted to lock myself into my hotel bathroom, since it didn't have any windows.

I still had to go everywhere with the team, and make it look as though nothing were wrong, even though I was always expecting to hear that muffled shot. Now I remembered all the warnings I had been given about Chicago being the city of gangsters, where at any instant, you might get a slug or two from a Colt automatic or a submachine gun. Perhaps it was that elegant gentleman standing over there, or the man by the stairs, or – I really didn't care for the idea that somebody was planning to kill me.

Fortunately, the telephone call was nothing but an ugly practical joke, an attempt to rattle us and spoil our stay. The scare may have accomplished the former, but not the latter.

I received a few more threats during my other four or five tours of the United States. I tried not to take them very seriously, but each time, I had the feeling there was someone deep in the pit of my stomach, scratching me with a piece of glass. So I was always assigned a bodyguard. On that first trip, it was a tall and modest man named Chuck, and on the other trips to America, I was accompanied by a strong, joyful mountain of a man named Bill. Bill was my perfect example of a typical American, and we became very good friends. Each time I came to the States, I would look for him as soon as the plane landed. The hatch would open, I would step outside and there he would be, smiling back at me.

It took me a while to understand that Americans enjoyed remarks like, 'Wow, what a big boy you are,' and that they almost *expected* a star to be feisty and capricious. As a result, I indulged myself in a childish whim the one time I arrived in the States, and Bill was not there to meet me. Instead, I saw an unfamiliar man coming up the steps of the plane.

'Hello, Olga,' he said pleasantly.

I froze in my tracks, blocking the passengers behind me. I was so caught off-guard that I found myself saying, 'I want Bill!' I realized as soon as I said it that it was a selfish reaction, but I wanted to see Bill.

And wouldn't you know, less than three hours later, my beloved Bill came running up to me, mopping perspiration from his forehead. I don't know where he had come from. But I have to admit that I was very happy to see him.

That occasion was particularly dramatic, but I know that working as my bodyguard was never an easy job. From the moment I stepped out of the airplane, he would become my shadow. Day and night, he would scan the area with his sharp eyes, ready to protect me from danger. Wherever I went – work-outs, shopping, performances – I could be sure that he would be right next to me, watching everything around us with those unblinking eyes.

I don't think he knew anything about me as a gymnast, because he never got a chance to see any of my shows. When I went to the podium, he would take a position near by, usually squatting, and watch the audience the entire time. When I moved to the next apparatus, he would move, too.

He followed me from bus, to plane, to bus, to plane, as we constantly travelled to different cities. I was not allowed to go into my hotel room until he had checked every inch – the windows, the closets, under the bed, everywhere. Then he would shout, 'Okay!' and come out to the corridor to get my bags.

Two police officers were stationed outside my room around the clock, and Bill stayed in an adjacent room. If I accidentally dropped a clothes brush on the floor or made too loud a sound closing the wardrobe, Bill would instantly appear on the threshold, holding his automatic pistol in outstretched hands.

In one city, I think it was Buffalo, I did something I still feel guilty about. I escaped from my hotel. Actually, I wasn't even trying to get away. I just came out of my room and walked down the hall, passing the two police officers. They were so deep in conversation that they didn't even notice me go by.

So I went outside, amused that I had managed to fool the cops. It was the first time I had ever been totally on my own in the States, and I walked down the street, whistling to myself and enjoying the day.

Then I heard a police siren and a car screeched to a stop right in front of me. Bill jumped out, so angry that I almost didn't recognize him. He grabbed the arrogant little gymnastics star and yanked her unceremoniously into the car.

I felt terrible about the whole thing and apologized profusely, promising that I would never, *ever* do it again. *Ever*.

After that, I had learned my lesson, and we never quarrelled again.

People always asked me what I liked best in America. Disneyland, of course! Remember, I was still pretty young. When I came out of the White House after meeting the President, I was quickly surrounded by reporters.

'How did you like it in there?' they asked.

'Well . . .' I had to be honest. 'Disneyland impressed me much more.'

I wasn't trying to be coy, or difficult. Well, okay, maybe just a little. But, I really did, and still do, love Disneyland. When I finally got a chance, many years later, to take my son Richard there, I watched his delighted little face and remembered my own first trip to that magical place.

When it came time to leave the United States and go back home, I always hated to go. I would be taking back my joyful memories of America and its people – simple, cordial, open-hearted, easy-going, and optimistic.

I never left without wondering when, and if, I would be able to come back.

Chapter Twelve

Unfortunately, the American tour did not bring our string of exhibitions to an end. We were on the road a great deal, and I wasn't able to concentrate on my own training in Grodno. It was already April, and the 1974 Varna World Championships were just over a year away. America had been good for my ego, but our trips to places like Denmark and London were not as rewarding for me. I was always tired, and could not seem to bring back the light feeling in my body that had been there in Munich. There, every movement had seemed as natural and easy as breathing.

We invariably got great receptions, but after being in the United States, nothing else seemed good enough.

I don't *think* I had contracted 'star disease'. Sometimes I was a little difficult, but I suspect I was just trying to amuse myself. One has to live with one's character and mine, as you've probably noticed, is not always of the best quality. I'm afraid I have been uncontrollable and a bit nasty from the moment I was born.

During those trips, it was obvious that the Sports Committee had realized that the success of our exhibitions was like printing banknotes. So they pushed us even harder. We no longer soared and leapt gracefully. We worked. We *slaved*.

Exhibition performances were especially trying when there was Coca-Cola and popcorn around. It was torture because we were all dieting. I could see the audience sitting out there, chewing and guzzling, and my mouth would be watering so much that it was hard to concentrate. I also thought that when people were eating, they didn't pay attention to what we were doing, and that hurt.

When I looked around the arena before my performances, I got upset if I saw any empty seats. I gave them everything I had, and I wanted every heart out there to be mine. I was working so hard, and I really wanted to be appreciated. Maybe I *did* have a touch of 'star disease'.

After touring for weeks on end, I was so tired I felt as though I couldn't do anything. Just looking at the apparatus made me sick. I felt nothing but apathy, anger and helplessness. Even so, I still had to go out and try to do my best. I owed that to the audiences.

While we were in Copenhagen, something happened that I will remember for the rest of my life. Ren hit me for the first time. Hit me *hard*.

It all went back to the time when Tamara Lazakovich first taught me to smoke, and Ren started noticing that sometimes I smelled like tobacco. We made a deal: if he ever caught me with a cigarette, I would pay him a fine of 100 roubles. He had the advantage because I was never allowed to lock my door. I would be lying there, reading, and suddenly the door would fly open and Ren would be standing there like a cat on the hunt.

'Are you smoking?' he would demand, and almost seem disappointed when he saw that I wasn't. 'Well, okay. . .'

Once in Grodno, I *was* smoking with a couple of other girls, but I had left the room just before he burst in. My two friends were taught an unwanted lesson because he went out and bought a pack of viciously strong cigarettes, 'Byelomorkanal', and made them smoke the entire pack in front of him. The result was that an ambulance had to be called for one of the girls, and neither of them went near a cigarette ever again.

I was never a serious smoker. I would just have one or two a day, after my work-outs. Probably the main reason I did it was because I wasn't supposed to. An athlete's life is filled with 'do nots', and I was rebelling. On top of that, I had to watch my weight very carefully, and after work-outs I was always so hungry! Puffing a cigarette often helped to dull my hunger pangs.

Besides, I desperately wanted to outsmart Ren. He always pushed me so hard that I had to allow myself the pleasure of that cigarette. I got very good at concealing them. In fact, he never found the hiding place in my Grodno apartment – in the seat of one of the kitchen stools. When I heard him coming in, I would quickly hide my treasure inside that stool, and no matter how hard he looked, he always left full of suspicions, but empty-handed.

His struggle to keep me from eating cakes was equally relentless. I was not permitted to have any, but I loved them so much! I would spread them on a piece of black bread (to reduce the threat of putting on weight) and gobble them down. My mother was aware of this weakness of mine, and whenever I was in hospital with an injury, she would stealthily smuggle small pieces in to me.

Ren did pretty well in his efforts to keep me away from cakes. Once, when I was twelve, he bought me a big one. I really couldn't believe my eyes. For two days straight, I ate nothing but that cake. Tea and cake, coffee and cake, tea and cake. . . . Eventually, the taste of cake was so sickening that I stopped.

My passion for that delicacy remained dormant for the next twenty-three years. Then, when I was thirty-five years old and had settled in the United States, I decided to take the risk. It seems funny that I ate my first slice where no one else could see me. And you know what? Once again, I decided that cake was great!

Anyway, the night Ren hit me for the first time, I was lying in my Copenhagen hotel room, flicking through a pornographic magazine I had begged the boys on the men's gymnastics team to lend me. I knew so very little about sex, and I just had to satisfy my curiosity.

As usual, the door was unlocked. Suddenly, Ren burst in with his usual predatory look.

'What did you put under that pillow?' he bellowed.

I felt very ashamed and couldn't look at him. He was a *man*, after all. Besides, I had only been curious. . .

He pushed me off the bed, reached under the pillow, and yanked the magazine out.

'Slut!' he said, angrier than I had ever seen him. 'So that's what you were doing!'

Nobody talks to me like that, and I stiffened, ready to shout back at him. Before I could, he started beating me, shaking me violently and ripping my clothes into shreds, while I stood as still as a statue. When he finally calmed down a little, I looked at him disdainfully.

I just bought this shirt today,' I said, spitting the words out. 'Tomorrow, you'll buy me two to replace this one.'

He stared at me, his eyes wide, and then tore out of the room.

I know he was furious because he thought he had finally proved one of his many suspicions, but what he had done to me was unforgivable.

Mothers and doctors know that the body goes through some physiological changes between the ages of thirteen and seventeen. A coach who had trained several female gymnasts in the past must also have been aware of that. The only one who was completely *ignorant* was me. My figure did not start to fill out until I was nineteen, apparently as a result of the draconian regime of my work-outs and starvation diet. My body had not received the elementary vitamins and minerals it needed to develop normally.

Many years later, worried about my liver, I consulted an American doctor, who said, 'Ms Korbut, you simply require a normal diet. It looks like you spent your entire childhood starving.'

I did.

Anyway, Ren had noticed the changes in my figure, and decided that I was stealing time from gymnastics to indulge in sex. When he found the magazine, he was convinced that he was right. And so, he beat me up.

We had another, similar conflict a short time later, when I got my period for the first time. Thinking I had sustained a serious internal injury while practicing on the uneven bars, I turned to one of my older and more experienced friends for advice. The woman laughed, and put her arm around my shoulders.

'How silly you are,' she said. 'You're only growing up. It's perfectly normal.'

To celebrate the good news, we went to the hotel restaurant where I said to myself, what the heck, and ate as much as I wanted. Later that night, a timid lieutenant came up to our table.

'May I invite you to dance?' he asked.

It was the first time in my life a man had ever asked me to dance!

All that happiness was short-lived. When Ren found out, he beat me up again, calling me a couple of dozen names borrowed from some dark cellar of the Russian language. The most printable one was 'Tart!'

He also punched me on several other occasions. One of the times was back at the gym in Grodno. We had just started training under a new system he had devised, where I had to spend a week perfecting an element and then be examined on it. I had been preparing for an exam on the beam when Ren gathered the whole group together, and motioned for me to come over.

'Go to the bars,' he ordered. 'Show them how it's done.'

'I can't, Renald Ivanovich,' I said. 'I've been preparing for the beam.'

'What's the matter, do you have trouble hearing?' he asked, obviously enraged. He wanted to demonstrate to the other girls both his authority and the fruits of his labour.

I didn't know what to say since I really couldn't go over to the bars and do the new element right away like that.

Without another word, he stepped up to me and cracked me across the side of the head. He is not a very big man, but he was more than strong enough to take on a girl my size. The punch was so hard that it ruptured the membrane in my ear. He had no time even to call an ambulance because my sister Ludmilla, who was also a student of his at that time, jumped on him, digging her fingernails into his body. As far as I can remember, they were both screaming – one from pain, the other from hatred.

Normally, he would punch me away from witnesses: in the corner, behind the piano, wherever. When my mother asked who had given me those bruises, I would look at her with my best innocent expression and say, 'I hit the bars.' Inside, I would be screaming, Mommy, the uneven bars never leave black eyes on a gymnast. . .

To this day, my mother hates Ren bitterly.

Before that night in Copenhagen, Ren would never have dared to touch me with a finger, and now he was like a watchdog who had been let off his chain.

We had another bad scene in Copenhagen during that same trip to Denmark. He and I were sitting in a small café, having our evening coffee. For a long time, neither of us spoke. Ren would start to say something, then seem to have second thoughts and stop. I just sat there, waiting. I was feeling very guilty because I felt I was going to go to pieces every time I approached the apparatus, and I couldn't understand what was wrong with me.

'Olga,' he said finally. 'Before, I just advised you to leave gymnastics. Now, I'm demanding that you do it. It's over for you. You've ceased to exist. The only thing that's left is Olga Korbut's myth. You have no desire, not a drop. You exhausted yourself completely in Munich.'

Maybe, maybe not. I didn't say anything.

'Believe me,' he went on, 'nobody lives in sports for long. Quit in glory, not disgrace. You've done a lot. Few people would be able to achieve what you did. You were born to be a soloist, not a chorus singer. You are no longer a good soloist. I'm begging you, quit now.'

I did not argue. I remained quiet, no emotions on the surface. Was he right? Should I agree with him? Not on your life! If only I had broken with him when he had first begun sowing the seeds of uncertainty in me. The seeds were now growing out of control. All I wanted, as Ren well knew, was the chance to finish my gymnastics career normally, at the 1976 Olympic Games in Montréal.

'No,' I said.

He shrugged. 'You won't make it. They'll throw you away like a mangy cat. Like refuse that belongs in a trash can. You should leave now. This is your last tour.'

'I don't want to quit,' I said.

It was a strange conversation. Neither of us had raised our voices even once. We were discussing dreadful things, but in a tired, matter-of-fact, almost disinterested way.

'You think you'll get a gold in Montréal?' He smirked at me. 'I bet you 1000 roubles that you won't. If you do, I'll give you a grand.'

I looked him right in the eye. 'You're on,' I said.

That conversation may have been one of his coach's tricks, trying to infuriate me so that I would start performing wonders, out of spite. Then again, he may simply have realized that I would never be able to surpass the Munich Olga. I guess I knew that too. Maybe he wanted me off the podium so that I would not repeat other gymnasts' mistakes of staying in the game too long. But I wanted to continue performing, and show what I could do in front of people who would enjoy it.

So far, no one has ever asked me why I didn't quit sooner. The only thing I have been asked is, 'Why did you quit so early?'

After all those exhibitions, in addition to my problems with Ren, my feelings of doubt and apathy only increased. However, by July 1973, I felt calmer and well rested. My zest for life seemed to return, and I was regaining my former level of fitness.

In August, I won the combined events at the Moscow Universiad, and Tourischeva placed second. I was no longer satisfied with my role of the elf behind the queen's back, and I had pushed her from the throne. I wanted to be the queen myself. In addition to the All-Round medal, I also took three golds in the individual events.

In October of that same year, I went to the European Championships in London. Crowds came to see the famous Korbut, and I would see posters on the streets reading, 'It's Happened! Olga on the Banks of the Thames!' Unfortunately, I disappointed all of those fans because I lost. Risk and setbacks are inevitable when you do the kind of gymnastics I did. I hope the fans realized that, even though I felt like weeping when I did not live up to their expectations.

On the last day of that event, I had a lead on Tourischeva. Then I had to drop out because of an injured ankle. After my first attempt at the vault, I felt an excruciating pain and literally crawled to the podium. I climbed up on a chair, and looked at my swollen foot. There was no way that I could continue. In the individual All-Round finals, half of a programme did not count, so I had to content myself with a silver medal. I am convinced that the inhuman loads we were given while slaving to fatten the Sports Committee's hard-currency account had a lot to do with my increasingly frequent injuries.

Exhibitions, exhibitions, exhibitions . . They made me sick! Ren didn't even bother trying to bargain with the National Team leadership to reduce my participation. He also demanded that I continue to perform new elements at each competition, complicated and unusual elements that no one else had ever executed before. I performed them reasonably well, but I did not have enough time to *master* them, so my risk of further injuries was enormous.

My team-mates could use the exhibitions as additional training for their soft and quiet routines, but I couldn't practise my raw moves in front of an audience because I couldn't afford to fall off the apparatus. I didn't want to lose the admiration of those fans.

So I had to learn all those new stunts in a hurry. The careful, scrupulous and consistent Renald Knysh I had always known was gone. In his place was a man who wanted to be known as the world's best coach, without lifting a finger to create a safe and healthy atmosphere for his pupil's training. If anything, he seemed to be working *against* that.

The Sports Committee was not even vaguely concerned about me. As long as I worked hard during those exhibitions so that they could fatten their coffers, they were satisfied. If asked about my future, I think they would have said, 'Screw her, that's her problem.' I would not be surprised at all to have heard the cynical sports administrators use those exact words.

Ren and I were now rushing to prepare a new, revolutionary vault. Ren called it the '360-plus-360'. It consisted of a

360-degree turn in the first flight, prior to push-off, and another 360-degree pirouette in the second flight phase, before landing.

Nobody had ever even attempted such a thing. A full turn before pushing off the horse was hard to imagine. Later, I discovered that one gymnastics theoretician had even written a dissertation, and received a scholar's degree, for proving scientifically that such an element was unfeasible.

To tell the truth, when Ren explained what he wanted me to do, I felt a chill of fear. People used to call me fearless, but the fear never really left me. I just learned how to control it. Ren had prepared for the attempt quite carefully, but time was running short. Now *I* was the one who wanted to do the old 'twenty times, flawlessly' routine, but Ren was in a hurry. An almost compulsive hurry. One minute, he would be attentive and helpful, and the next, he would callously mistreat me. In the past, I had hated spending a year or more on the same element to make each tiny component utterly familiar, but now I was *striving* for that goal.

And Ren wasn't.

The small crack in our relationship had now become a great chasm. Our partnership had broken apart and now the unthinkable happened. He walked out! We didn't quarrel, shout or throw accusations at each other. We just separated, like an intelligent married couple with irreconcilable differences, who finally decide not to torture each other any more by continuing the farce.

It was over. The coach I had known for most of my life – my best friend, and my worst enemy – was gone.

Chapter Thirteen

Even now, I am not sure how I feel about Renald Knysh. We spent so much time together, both good times and bad, and knew each other better than anyone else. I know that we parted for many reasons, but one of the main ones was that I was becoming an adult, with my own opinions and ways of doing things. I was no longer a piece of modelling clay for his experiments. When he was angry, he would always shout, 'I can mould a thousand girls like you! You're an obstacle! A waste of my time!' Now he decided to look for new, more pliable material. He was only satisfied when he could be the master, not an equal partner.

I was relieved that we had finally gone our separate ways, but it was also very difficult. I resented him for hurting me during a period when I really needed his help. I was so overworked because of those exhibitions, and so tired.

Even then, despite his official departure, he was still drawn back to me. In the middle of the night, the telephone would ring in my hotel room, in London or wherever else I happened to be on tour.

'Hi, it's me,' he would say. 'How are you doing?'

'So far, so good,' I would answer.

We would have a brief, civil conversation, and then, just as abruptly, he would be gone from my life for another six months. I could not seem to cut him off permanently, and if I needed help with something, I would usually end up calling him. It is very hard to disown someone you love.

My next coach was Tamara Stepanovna Alexayeva, one of Ren's former students. She had been a very talented and promising gymnast, whose career was cut short by a freak injury. She left the National Team just before the Tokyo Olympics, and was never able to return to competition. After that, she became a coach – Ren's 'right hand' in the gym and, for a while, his companion outside it. Now, she was my coach.

We went to Leselidze, and enthusiastically plunged into work. I was so intent on showing Ren that I did not need him in order to do well that I was oblivious to everything else, even the proximity of my beloved Black Sea. I wanted to hurt Ren for his betrayal, and achieving great things would be the best revenge. My new coach and I would polish the diamond Ren had discovered into perfection.

Tamara Alexayeva was a quiet and intelligent woman, and not all that happy with my wild character. But every day, she would say in her soft and friendly voice, 'Come for tomorrow's work-out, please. I'll be waiting for you.' I doubt if she realized how much those simple kind words meant to me during that chaotic time of my life. Instead of being coach and student, we were more like friends. It was a nice change.

We practised daily to get ready for the Varna Championships. A month before the world meet, we went to the National Championship in Vilnius. I had a run-in with Latynina there, who was up to her usual hypocritical tricks. I really dislike people who are 'two-faced', and the sweet fake smiles she always gave me were infuriating.

In Vilnius, Tamara and I wanted to test the new, scientifically unfeasible vault. We contacted Latynina in advance, because there was a rule in the National Championship code which stipulated that in the finals of the vault, the gymnast was to make two attempts, with a different group structure exercise in each. But our two vaults were from the same group, the main difference being the degree of difficulty. (It is worth mentioning that the international code did not have that ridiculous rule.)

'Larissa Semyenovna, we are planning to do a new vault in Vilnius, the 360-plus-360,' we told her. 'It belongs to the same structure group, but it is very complicated and we are trying to get ready for Varna. We'd like to give it a try.'

'I don't have anything against that,' Latynina replied. 'Keep on working.'

Naturally, we felt reassured. But when we got to the National Championships, a few minutes before the vaulting finals, she came up to Tamara.

'Tell Olga to perform some other vault,' she said.

Tamara, who was very sensitive, started trembling. 'What?' she asked. 'Why? You promised, remember? There are only three minutes left before she has to vault!'

Latynina smiled her smile. 'That's the rule,' she said. 'You know it perfectly well.'

While this was going on, I was on the other side of the hall and could not hear the conversation. But when I saw them talking, I got a nasty suspicion, and hurried over to Tamara as soon as Latynina walked away.

'What's the matter?' I asked. 'What were you talking about?'

'Nothing,' Tamara said. 'Everything is fine.'

If everything was so fine, why she was crying?

Tamara repeated the entire conversation to me and, feeling my insides boiling, I knew that I was about to erupt. I went over to confront Latynina myself, doing my best to stay under control.

'What's the problem, Larissa?' I asked, too calmly.

'Ah, well, you see, I myself have no objections, but referee Minina is against your vault,' Larissa explained. 'She thinks it should be credited with zero points.'

I found Minina, and erupted all over *her* instead.

'What do you mean?' the referee asked, completely surprised. 'I don't mind at all. You can jump whatever you want. It was Latynina who asked us not to credit your second vault.'

Why had I ever suspected otherwise? I stormed back over to Latynina.

'To hell with you!' I shouted. 'I won't do any vault at all!' Then I went straight to the locker room, my formerly warm muscles now stiff and shaking with anger.

Out in the performance hall, it had become very quiet. I was no longer a little girl whose absence would go unnoticed; I was a major gymnast, with a large following. There were reporters everywhere, including members of the foreign press, and Latynina was not about to antagonize or lose face in front of them.

Within a few minutes, she had sent a delegation into the locker room to ask me to come back out. When I refused, Latynina came in herself, finding me on a training table, with Tamara and our masseuse trying to relax my rigid muscles.

'Olga, I've arranged everything,' Latynina said grandly. 'The second vault will also be credited.'

I ignored her, and Tamara and the masseuse looked at each other.

'Will you do the vault?' Tamara asked finally. 'Please, for me?'

I thought about it, then nodded, and got off the table.

So, I did my vaults – both the 360-plus-360, and an even more unusual 540-plus-180 that Tamara and I had been preparing secretly. They were very successful, and even though Tourischeva's coach Rastorotski had arranged with Latynina for her to win the gold in vault, I took it instead.

Boy, do I hate 'arrangements' like that! It was not, of course, the first time I had heard about judges being bribed, nor would it be the last. Tourischeva must have been feeling some pressure after she saw my 360-plus-360, because at the end of the second flight phase in her next vault, she landed on all fours. I felt sorry for her, but if she was really a champion, she should have proved it, and won the titles on her own. No true champion would ever allow a victory to be 'arranged'.

Soon, it was October, and time for the World Championships. My work with Tamara had been going very well, and I felt more prepared than I ever had. Ren may have thought that I had peaked in Munich, but as far as I'm concerned, the top performances of my career were at Varna. I felt an unprecedented sense of confidence, and each of my routines was truly flawless. I have never been better, before or since.

To my surprise, Ren was among the spectators at Varna. Had he come to see me fail, or to share in my success? After my warm-up, he beckoned to me and I reluctantly went over.

'You're in excellent shape, Olga,' he said with his usual lack of small talk, 'but you won't win this championship. Tourischeva will.'

I stared at him. 'But why? I'm more ready than I've ever been!'

'I know,' he said. 'But they won't give you a chance. So don't get upset about it. Just go on and do everything you can do. But be prepared to lose.'

I assumed that he was probably lying to me, so I didn't worry. Apart from being in the best physical condition of my career, I had recently started doing 'auto-training' with a psychotherapist named Rodionov. He had been teaching me how to relax so that I would be able to go to sleep at the right time, to wake up when necessary, and to focus my mind before training or performing. These new concentration techniques had enhanced my confidence even more.

Our National Team won the team competitions easily, although the team from the German Democratic Republic gave us a few problems along the way. Then it was time for the All-Round individual competition. Even though I knew I had performed better than anyone else, I lost almost every event. When my scores came up, I fought off tears of resentment, while the audience supported me with boos and roars of indignation.

The only time I lost my temper outright was when I didn't get the gold for the uneven bars – my best apparatus. The gold was given to Zinke, a German athlete whose routine was neither original nor executed perfectly. When I saw the results, I went up to Yuri Titov, the leader of our delegation.

'This is ridiculous,' I told him. 'You saw yourself that I should have had the gold for the uneven bars. We should file a protest.'

'Yes, I saw,' he said. 'We should not file a protest.'

How could my *own* team leadership do this to me? I decided to appeal to his greedy side. 'But we're losing a medal! How come we shouldn't protest?'

'Relax, Olga,' he said, without even looking over at me. 'We're not losing anything.'

Now I got it. Ludmilla Tourischeva was supposed to be retiring from the sport soon, and they wanted her to leave in a beautiful way, a Socialist way. She would go out on top, and it would be a glorious farewell. It didn't matter how hard all of the athletes worked – pulling ligaments in our young bodies, breaking bones, and giving up anything resembling normal lives. Behind our backs, the adults who ran the sport treated us like pawns on a chessboard, deciding who would win or lose for their own selfish reasons.

In any event, it turned out that our team had 'given away' first place on the bars to Zinke; while in return, Tourischeva would receive the gold in the floor exercise. Each of the winners had been selected before we even set foot on the podium. It wasn't much consolation when one of the German judges (ours got off scot-free) was later disqualified with great fanfare – especially when that very same judge returned to sit on the panel of judges at the Olympic Games in Montréal.

I still can't believe that anyone would want to distribute titles in advance. It has always been difficult to bribe Western judges, but it was no problem with the judges from the Socialist countries. There was a joke at the time: when a rooster crows in Moscow, people in Prague (Berlin, Warsaw, etc.) say 'Good morning'. Incidentally, this 'system' was also practised in sports other than gymnastics.

If, for some reason, the Soviet athletes did not win a majority of the medals at a competition, the officials of the sports federations would simply point out that the teams of the Socialist camp had won so many medals, compared with the lower number of medals won by Western athletes. It was important that there always be a Socialist victory over capitalism. That is such a stupid attitude! Sports are supposed to unite people, not serve as a method to divide them.

What happened at Varna with the uneven bars was bad enough, but the judges really blew it on my vault.

I had been having trouble with it the day before, so on the morning of the finals, Tamara and I decided that I should perform only one simple, flawless pirouette. Immediately before my turn, I couldn't help searching the crowd for Ren. Even though we were no longer working together, I wanted to see that familiar confidence in his eyes. He was waving his hands frantically at me, and all I could make out was that he was saying, 'Sharper! Don't fidget!'

Okay. I took a deep breath, and did the vault. The scoreboard read only 9.70. Well, what else could I have expected for such a simple vault? To win the gold, I needed a 9.80, and that elementary vault just wasn't going to do it. I looked over at Ren, begging him for advice with my eyes. He nodded, giving me the green light to do the 360-plus-360.

I ran down towards the vault, and there it was, that blessed moment when time and movement break down into familiar molecules and atoms. Take-off! Turn! Push-off! Turn! Inside my head, I could hear Ren's grouchy advice from our original practice sessions: 'After the push-off, turn and try to land on your back. Then you'll land perfectly. If you think about landing on your feet, you'll surely be carried forward, and when you land, you'll run ahead.'

I did my best to follow that advice during the second flight, and it helped. I landed perfectly, with my legs knee-deep in the matting.

Wow, that was great! One of the best I had ever done!

The scoreboard flashed 9.80, which was a humiliatingly low score for such a fantastic vault. It was high enough for me to win the gold.

There was something unfamiliar about the applause I was getting, and when I turned around, I saw that all of the other gymnasts on the floor were also clapping and cheering.

'Spectators are very emotional,' Ren had always said. 'It's easy to cheat them with something flashy. But if you ever manage to impress and amaze your colleagues, then you may consider yourself a Master of the Sport, not simply a craftsman.'

My colleagues – the other gymnasts – were giving me a standing ovation.

It may be the best compliment I have ever received.

When I decided to write this book, I knew that Ren had always kept journals during the time we had worked together, so I went to him and asked to borrow his notes. After some wavering, he said that he had lost them. I guess he just didn't want to give them to me. Maybe he's saving them for a book of his own.

But once, I did get a chance to look at the diary he kept during the World Championships at Varna. He had written the notes for his own eyes, so I know that they were honest.

'October 19, 1974,' he had written. 'Varna (before the World Championship)... Olga is alone in the gym (our other girls didn't come – it's a day off). She worked a dismount from the beam. Very poor. I'm worried about it. Told her to practise the dismount more – she refused. Had to tell her it was the weakest part of her routine. She flared up: 'Don't try to frighten me!' But repeated the dismount about thirty times. It looked better.

'FE (Floor Exercise) Several times salto and separate elements. Ordered her to do a new dismount. She'll have to perform it in the finals. It will be named after her, the 'Korbut Dismount'. All the guys grabbed their cameras at once.

'On the UPB (Uneven Parallel Bars) two compulsory routines – very well, the Japanese even gasped. On the 360-degree vault, three times – not bad, but not as good as at home. 360-plus-360-well done, although arms were slightly bent – wild applause. The whole Japanese team was so impressed, they sat down on the floor. Another attempted, very poor – started the second turn too early, without a pause. Compulsory – excellent! Everybody's going crazy, a dozen guys shooting with their cameras...'

If he had treated me the way he wrote about me, our partnership might never have ended.

Chapter Fourteen

After Varna, I began to realize that I wasn't going to be this strong and skilled for much longer. I was twenty years old now, and it was getting harder to endure those numerous exhibition tours. Australia, the USA, Singapore, Great Britain, back to the USA – I was getting very tired. I was tired of performing, and *very* tired of earning money for the fat big-shots on the Sports Committee. Once again, I was feeling that terrible weight of depression and apathy.

I was unable to train hard, and Tamara Alexayeva would just wince. I was starting to get a little scared myself. How much longer was I going to be able to go on like this?

Still, a few good things happened. I was invited to San Remo, a small Italian resort, where I was awarded a UNESCO 'Peace Envoy of 1974' Medal of Honour. At the same ceremony, Alain Delon, a famous European actor; Dr Christian Barnard, the surgeon who had performed the first human heart transplant; the sculptor Missino; and the singer Domenico Modounio also received Golden Tuning Fork awards. I was in pretty good company.

The ceremony was held in a magnificent theatre, and everybody who was anybody in the local area attended. By an ancient tradition, each laureate was suppose to perform some sort of number, and demonstrate a talent. What was I going to do? There were not going to be any apparatuses there.

Well, I wasn't about to sing in the presence of the great Domenico Modounio, so I decided to dance. But I was going to need a leotard, and I hadn't brought one along because no one had told me that I had to participate in the 'talent' show. Unfortunately, it was Saturday, and all the shops in San Remo were closed.

'I know,' suggested one of the officials. 'We have a store which is open seven days a week, and you'll probably be able to find a swimsuit there.'

I shrugged. 'Great. Let's go.'

'Well . . .' the woman hesitated, 'the problem is, it is a sex shop, and while they sell swimsuits, the fabric is transparent.'

Oh. Well, did I have any other options? 'Let's go and take a look,' I said, blushing.

In the end, I bought two transparent swimsuits and stitched them together, creating a suit that was a little less risqué. It wasn't exactly a leotard I would normally wear around the gym, but it covered the essentials, so I would be able to go out on the stage without much embarrassment.

I was the first one scheduled to perform my act. Timidly, I sang a couple of bars from 'Kaleenka' to the orchestra conductor, who instantly understood what I needed. Then I showed the grand ladies in their mink coats and their companions in tuxedos a brief compilation from my floor exercises. I was extremely relieved when this was received with the usual enthusiasm. I had dreaded the thought of disgracing myself in front of the other honourees.

Delon came out and played a scene from a play, and Modounio, naturally, sang. But what were the surgeon and the sculptor going to do?

Barnard brought out a guitar, touched its strings with his strong fingers, and the hall was filled with an unexpectedly beautiful, velvety voice. The audience was delirious with excitement, and demanded an encore.

'I'm sorry,' the great surgeon said shyly. 'I'd be happy to sing more, but I'm afraid that was the only song I know.'

Then, Missino came out and did a stand-up routine, telling the audience funny stories about his life. It was really a hoot.

The next day, Missino invited me to his studio in Milan for an hour or two. There, while I sat and watched in amazement, he transformed a shapeless piece of clay into a perfect likeness of me. I was very impressed. Ren had always talked

126

about my being material in his brilliant hands but he didn't have anything on Missino.

When I met Alain Delon at the reception, I felt unusually shy, and very aware of myself as a woman. This was not a familiar feeling for me, and I was tongue-tied. I don't think it was his celebrity that rattled me – after all, I was pretty popular myself! Maybe it had something to do with how handsome he was. . .

During our dance together, the crowd of reporters made it very hard for us to move.

'Kiss each other!' the most arrogant one insisted.

'We'll kiss when we feel like it,' Alain said pleasantly. 'Not when you ask.'

We did our best to talk to each other, using the only language we had in common – English.

'Your English is very poor, Olga,' he told me.

'And your Russian is zero, Alain,' I told him.

Maybe he didn't sense anything at all, but some feelings normally suppressed by the difficult regimen of my work were certainly rising in me. Doctors have since studied the phenomenon of retarded development in women's gymnastics, and found it almost universal. Either way, a part of myself I didn't know very well was finally starting to wake up.

The only disappointing aspect of being in San Remo was that Larissa Latynina had accompanied me.

'They invited both of us,' she explained.

Sure.

But when it was time to give me my medal, they announced that 'The Medal "Peace Envoy of 1974" is awarded to the coach of the magnificent Olga Korbut, Larissa Latynina.'

What? My coach? I had assumed that she was invited because she was the senior coach of the National Team. Wait, no. Surely, this could not be another deception. Maybe she was just going to accept the Golden Tuning Fork, and then give it to Ren later. He and I may have had our problems, but fair was fair.

Those were naïve hopes on my part. She gave him nothing. When UNESCO had informed Moscow about the awards being presented to Olga Korbut and her coach, the Sports Committee decided that some mere provincial upstart did not deserve such a prestigious honour. It would be much more appropriate for the senior coach of the USSR National Team to receive the medal instead. So, they sent UNESCO Latynina's name along with mine.

This had happened before. Once, Ren was awarded a very rare medal in the Soviet Union, the Golden Star for Coaching. He received the certificate and the 1000 roubles that came with the award, but the actual Golden Star disappeared into the collection of some unscrupulous member of the Sports Committee. How typical.

Another time, I was given a car during one of my tours of the United States. It was a gorgeous red Chevrolet and I was very excited. Automobiles are one of my great passions. Rick Appleman, the tour's organizer, approached the ambassador of the USSR first.

'Is it okay if we present Olga Korbut with an automobile and have it shipped to the Soviet Union?' he asked.

'No problem,' the ambassador assured him.

But the car was never sent because when Rick mentioned the plan to Titov, the chairman of the Sports Committee, Titov's response was, 'No! By no means!'

I never did get that car, and I have always resented it. How would my driving around in a Chevrolet have harmed my country? Depriving me of that generous gift seemed like an unnecessary cruelty.

One final example of the Sports Committee's boorish behaviour was when I happened to be in Moscow several years ago, and ran into Titov.

'Oh, here.' He thrust something into my hands. 'I guess this is yours.'

It was a Beatles Gold Record, inscribed 'To the Best Female Athlete of 1972'. It was scratched and twisted, and the glass had been broken out of the frame as though someone had kicked it. I felt so offended and helpless that I just stood there and cried. Later, I was able to have the record restored, but it wasn't the same.

*

Now, it was the second half of 1975. The European Championship, The Spartakiad of the Peoples of the USSR, and the World Cup were all approaching fast. More importantly, the Montréal Olympics were only a year away.

I hurt my ankle again, and was unable to go to the European Cup in Norway. It was the same ankle I had damaged so badly at the Championship in London, and I was frustrated and depressed by reinjuring it.

At that competition, for the first time, our team experienced a shattering defeat. A thirteen-year-old named Nadia Comaneci of Roumania had come out of nowhere and stolen the show. One of our athletes, Nelli Kim, placed second, and the ever-present Tourischeva came third.

Later, when I watched the films from a national Roumanian Championship, I saw that although Nadia was a really great gymnast, there were a lot of faults in her routines. Sitting in front of the television set, I mentally deducted decimal point after decimal point from the score for each of her mistakes. I was flabbergasted when I saw the judges unanimously give her a 10.00. In the past, *nobody* could have received a mark like that. What was wrong with the judges? Hadn't they seen the obvious errors? If they were giving her a 10.00 for *that*, then I should have been getting *12.00s* in my time.

Later, I understood the cunning strategy the Roumanians were using. The purpose of those promotional tapes, showing the flood of 10.00 marks, was to bring pressure on the judges in the forthcoming Olympics. Well, they certainly got the desired result! From that moment on, there was an epidemic of 10.00 scores. It was crazy.

Let me stress again that I always thought that Comaneci was a very talented and gifted gymnast. Her main flaw was on her landings: she just wouldn't stand properly. Often, she wouldn't even deserve a 9.90, and she got 10.00s. I think she probably knows this herself.

She and I have never exactly been friends, but as she has got older, our relationship has improved. We really only see each other at competitions. At one time she wouldn't even say hello, but now she does. It's kind of funny though – when I run into her coach, he *still* won't speak to me.

My ankle was improving, and as I prepared for the World Cup, I started feeling better. But still, something was very wrong. I just didn't have any energy, and I was always exhausted.

Tamara was so worried that she went to Ren for advice. After one look at me, he immediately summoned some top doctors to examine me. They came to a very simple conclusion: I was suffering from total depression. They decided to give me injections of something called Ritabulin, which would stimulate my nervous system, but at the expense of the body's inner resources. In other words, it helped me exhaust myself even more efficiently.

At the time, it seemed like a good idea. It helped me return to my work. I was able to feel things again, see colours, and generally rejoin the human race.

Comaneci did not participate in the World Cup. The rumour was that she was hiding from us. Tourischeva won the All-Round competition and I came in second. I was able to take my revenge at the Spartakiad, where I both won the All-Round category, and was captain of the first-place Belorussian team.

Whenever I felt as if I was fading away again, the doctors would give me another injection of the medicine. It almost always helped. Part of my problem was that I still missed Ren. No matter how hard I tried, I just couldn't forget him, and I felt very lonely.

When Tamara and I realized that we could not work out a new double flip by ourselves, we went back to Grodno. Somehow, Ren was able to teach me how to do the move in one day. If nothing else, he is a very talented gymnastics coach.

By the time the Olympic Games started, I was better prepared technically than I had been before Munich or Varna. My old programmes had all been revised and improved, and my 360-plus-360 vault was perfect. On the beam, I had an interesting new connecting move: a flak, followed immediately by a back layout dive through a chest roll. I also had developed a very original dismount: a front flip with a 540-degree turn. In the floor exercises, I was doing the double flip that Ren had taught me in a single day, so everything should have been great.

It wasn't. Several days before the Games started, my ankle flared up again, and the Ritabulin stopped working. It went downhill from there.

When I analyse my defeat in Montréal, I think maybe the worst problem was my complete apathy. By the time I got halfway through the compulsory programme I wasn't just limping, but completely dragging my leg. I had to exclude most of my best elements from my routines, so I had no chance to win any of the individual competitions. My main reaction to all of this was complete indifference. Even the warm receptions I got from the audience didn't help.

Montréal was my downfall, and my disgrace. But it was also part of my life, and I can't pretend that it didn't happen.

Was I angry to see that the spectators had a new idol in Nadia Comaneci? No. That was the least of my problems. Maybe thanks to the struggles Ren and I had had with judges over the years, it was easier now for the new wave of gymnasts to get high scores. Whatever; my instinct was just to let it rest.

When the Games were over, I had won a team gold medal, and two silver medals for my bars and beam routines. I felt a little bitter, but I also felt very tired.

Remembering our angry bet, I went to Ren and silently handed him the gold medal I had taken away from the Montréal Games. He leaned forward to study the small yellow metal disc.

'That's not it,' he said scornfully. 'It's a team gold. Not a soloist's medal.'

I exploded, thrusting the glittering piece at him. 'And what is this?' I shouted. 'Isn't that a medal? *Isn't it?*'

'You've lost, Olga,' he said maliciously. 'Admit it. It isn't the 1000 roubles that bothers you. It's that you are not *the* "Munich Olga". You are just a "Montréal Olga".'

I fetched the 1000 roubles from home, and threw the money in his face. The iridescent bills spilled all over his spartan room.

'You have lost,' was all he said.

No, I had won. Getting to Montréal at all was itself a victory. I got there alone, without him, fighting injuries and depression every step of the way. Maybe I hadn't dazzled or amazed anyone this time, but I had won. Over whom? Maybe just myself.

For the next year, I participated in some insignificant competitions and exhibitions. I went to places like Malaysia and Iran. Most of the time, I felt too ill and tired to think about anything else. There was no way that I would be able to go on like this.

It was raining when we returned from Iran to Moscow. I sat on the steps at the entrance to the airport with large raindrops streaming down my face and shoulders. People were scampering about all around me, preoccupied with their own problems.

Where were they all going in such a hurry? Stop for a minute! I was giving it all up, and none of them would ever see Olga Korbut on the podium again. But no one stopped. I doubt that they even would have been interested.

When I reached Grodno, instead of going home, I went straight to the hospital. I had so many unusual symptoms that the doctors treated me for every possible infection simultaneously. It turned out that I was just completely exhausted and dehydrated. My body had finally given out. It was time to retire.

I disappeared from gymnastics, and no one even noticed.

Chapter Fifteen

I didn't know it yet, but a very good thing had already happened to me. In 1976, when I was going over to tour the United States with the Olympic team, the famous Belorussian pop group 'Pesnyary' was on the plane with us. They were as big in Russia as the Beatles were in the West. Obviously, I had heard of them, but I had never met any of the band members before.

Everyone on the plane was very cheerful and boisterous, although I was feeling a little down. The team wanted the band to sing for us, so the group chief handed Leonid Bortkevitch, the lead singer, a guitar, and asked him to do one of his beautiful, sad songs for us. But Leonid didn't seem to want to sing. In fact, he looked as sad as I felt, and I went over and sat next to him.

'What are you doing, just sitting here like this?' I asked. 'Let's talk.'

We didn't stop for the next six hours, talking about everything under the sun. I remember one particular thing I said.

'If I ever get married,' I told this fair-haired stranger, 'it will not be to a sportsman, an actor or a musician. I'm so tired of all this nerve-wracking hustle, moving around from one place to another. I want a normal family, and a normal life. I don't need much. I just want to stop travelling all the time.'

How could I know then that Fate had something else in store for me?

At the end of the trip, Leonid wrote his address and telephone number in my notebook.

'If you're ever in Minsk, give me a call,' he said.

'Sure,' I answered, and promptly forgot about the whole thing.

I ended up calling him exactly one year later, and we have been together ever since.

This seems a good moment to mention an earlier incident. During my first trip to America, years before, I had seen a beautiful wedding gown in the window of an Atlanta store. I was very young then, and had no plans to marry at that time, but I loved the dress so much that, after two days of changing my mind repeatedly, I decided to buy it with some of the per diem money I had saved up.

The dress was just gorgeous! The veil was made of Venetian lace, and the dress itself looked like snowflakes and camomiles sewn together. I was also amused by the idea that buying the dress would give the press something else to speculate about.

As it turned out, some American company had already purchased it for me before I got a chance to count my meagre finances. So now the dress was mine, and the reporters were full of wild guesses. Instead of important issues like inflation, disarmament and the energy crisis, the front page of many American newspapers that day carried a picture of me smiling, and holding the two splendid boxes.

For the next week, I was questioned constantly about my non-existent fiancé. Then, one day, to my horror, I discovered that my gown had been stolen from my room. The state police energetically investigated the case, and soon found the culprits. The dress was returned to me in front of a crowd of reporters and television cameras.

'Law enforcement in a country is characterized not by the presence of criminals, Miss Olga,' the officer in charge of the investigation said solemnly, 'but by the ability of the authorities to neutralize them.'

Once again, my dress and I made more than our share of headlines.

In the end, I brought the dress back to Grodno, and packed it away for the unknown future. Not only did I have no specific plans to marry, I didn't even have anyone in mind.

I was naturally familiar with 'Pesnyary', since the band had sold millions of records, but I wasn't particularly interested in them. I had seen them on television back in 1972 and I thought, this group is so *ugly*. Then I noticed Leonid, and I thought, well, that one is maybe okay, I could marry that one, he's not so bad. But I was just kidding.

Right before the Olympic Games, there was a record show on the radio, and Olympic Team members were supposed to call in and request songs. I called in, and asked for Pesnyary's song, 'Alesya', which was then very popular. It was a song about love, and Alesya was the girl's name. Leonid has since told me that when he heard me request their song, he figured that I really liked him, and he started paying more attention to my gymnastics. He had always watched the Olympics, but now he just started to watch me.

I like to tell *him* that I only requested 'Alesya' because I didn't know any other songs.

For the next few years, we often came close to meeting. We would be on the same train, or the same plane, and catch a glimpse of each other from afar, but we were never actually introduced. After the Olympics, Pesnyary was doing a concert at the same sports palace in Minsk where we were doing a gymnastics exhibition. He tells me he passed the stage where I was warming up, thinking, 'Well, she knows me, definitely, since she requested my song, and she'll look over at me and smile,' but I didn't. He was very disappointed, because I didn't even glance in his direction.

So, what made me call him finally, after a year?

Actually, I *was* planning to get married, and I wasn't sure whether or not I was doing the right thing. The man in question was also an athlete. I was not deeply in love with him, but I guess I thought that it was time for me to settle down. He was a very quiet, reasonable person, and my parents fully approved of him. They figured that his personality would calm me down, and serve as an antidote to my erratic tendencies. I, on the other hand, was uncertain whether I loved him, and sure that he did not love me. I think he had soberly calculated the pros and cons, and decided that I would be a good wife for him. It was all just a little too rational and calm.

But the date for the ceremony had already been set, and all my parents' preparations were in full swing. I tried to explain that I really wasn't sure if I should go through with it, but they just told me to be quiet.

Everything came to a head when my husband-to-be decided – without even asking my opinion first – that I would have to take his last name. I didn't like the way he was treating me, and I also didn't want to stop being Olga Korbut. I was *famous* for being Olga Korbut. Why should I have to change my name? I think it was his way of trying to control me, and I have always been a free person. I didn't want to be with someone who expected to have power over me.

I was lost; I didn't know what to do. So I left him and went off to Minsk. I didn't know who to call, or who I could talk to about my problems. I had completely forgotten about Leonid, or that I had his number. I had a girlfriend in Minsk, and so I looked through my address book for her phone number. I tried to call her, but she wasn't home.

Now, as it happened, her name began with 'A', and Leonid's surname begins with 'B'. I was flipping through my book, and I saw his name and thought, well, should I call him or not? I didn't really feel comfortable about the idea. For one thing, he was married. But he was also a very famous person, and I thought he might understand why I was so upset, and be able to give me some good advice.

So I picked up the phone. 'Lenya?' I said, when he answered, using his nickname. 'This is Olga Korbut.'

He seemed very surprised to hear from me, but also pleased, and instantly invited me to come over. I was accustomed to making all my own decisions, so I felt awkward about asking someone else for advice, but I decided to go. I was in a strange city, alone in a hotel room, and I had to talk to *someone*.

It took me about an hour and a half by bus to reach his home on the other side of the city. He told me later that he had decided that I wasn't going to show up, and that I had just been some 'star' playing a practical joke on him.

When he answered the door, he looked happy and uncertain.

'Is something wrong?' I asked.

He nodded, and motioned for me to come inside. We talked for a long time, sharing our sad stories. I had gone there because I needed to talk to someone, not because I had a romantic interest. After all, I knew that he was married, and therefore unavailable. But now he told me that since he and the band spent so much time on the road, his marriage had suffered greatly, and his wife was having an affair. In fact, she had just gone off to Sochi with her boyfriend. Leonid was very unhappy, but he had been raised to believe that divorce was wrong, so he was trapped.

Before that night, I never believed in love at first sight. Now I do. This was the first time I had ever *really* looked at him, and I liked what I saw. I told him about all *my* troubles, and I fell in love with the look in his eyes because he was so obviously, sincerely trying to help me. I think the two of us were truly meant to be together.

After that day, we met again a few more times, and once, I heard him talking on the phone to his mother.

'Mom, I'm going to get married,' he said.

'What about the other one?' his mother asked.

'Come on, don't pretend you don't know what she's been doing,' he said.

She admitted that she did, but then reminded him about how she and his father felt about divorce.

'I'm getting married, mother,' he said.

When he hung up, I looked over at him.

'I don't seem to remember,' I said. 'Have you asked *me* yet?'

He grinned. 'No. I just know that you are going to be my wife.'

And he was right.

His present wife, who was in love with her boyfriend, was not at all disappointed by this turn of events.

At last, that bridal gown I had brought from America was going to come in handy.

Lenya and I decided to go off to the country together, to get away from civilization for a while. We went to the little village where my father had grown up. (Both my parents had met him by now, and they liked him tremendously.) I had been to the country before, but being in love made me see everything differently. It was so beautiful there! We were in a part of Belorussia with very virgin land. There were forests, lakes and lots of picturesque scenery. Being in love made me really appreciate all this.

I introduced Lenya to horses, and we went riding together. We slept in the hay. We went fishing, and caught a bunch of crawfish, and it was just a fabulous trip.

We spent two weeks out there, and really learned a lot about each other. We both wondered how we had ever managed to live apart for so many years. Before, our lives had both revolved around travels, big cities, performances and success. Now, we had peace, beauty, Nature and love.

We got married on 7 January. We were planning to have a simple ceremony at home, with just our families and a few close friends in attendance. It didn't exactly work out that way.

I don't know how they got the information, but suddenly the press knew all about our plans. We had mentioned it once on a long-distance phone call, and I suppose the line was tapped. Besides, Pesnyary and I were both too famous for the news to stay hidden long.

A delegation of city leaders came to my mother to tell her that the wedding should be held at the huge, newly built Veras Restaurant. They told her that several hundred Western correspondents had already asked to come, although ultimately, only three were allowed to attend.

The wedding was a madhouse, and when it seemed as though the celebration was never going to end, we were 'kidnapped' by Mikhail Suponev, who was a Belorussian correspondent for the *Sovietski Sport*. He hid us at his house, so that we could avoid any further interruptions of our privacy.

By putting aside my per diem money over the years, I had managed to save quite a bit of money, and had a large collection of records, some stereo equipment, and several valuable rings, including a unique diamond spider with emeralds on its legs, which was worth about 20,000 roubles.

Well, our Grodno apartment was burgled that very first night after we got married. They took everything, including nearly all the awards and souvenirs I had accumulated during my gymnastics career. They even took the White House brooch President Nixon had given me. All my treasures were gone. The robbers completely cleaned us out.

To make matters worse, the apartment had been ransacked despite the fact that it was in the same building where some regional Party Committee bosses lived, and the entrance was, supposedly, always guarded by an armed militiaman. Strange, isn't it, that the robbers were able to get in anyway?

It took three years, but the thieves were finally caught when one of them stole something from the other and they had a violent quarrel. I couldn't believe it when the investigator told me that it had been two old friends of mine, Mikhalyuk and Ryabkov. The truth only sank in when I saw them in prison, bewildered and scared.

They were convicted at the trial, and given long sentences. To this day, I am still getting some compensation from them. But I would be much happier if they hadn't robbed us in the first place.

After my retirement, the USSR Council of Ministers decided to give me a monthly allowance of 300 roubles for the rest of my life, so I did not need a job at that point. I spent the beginning of our marriage resting and trying to regain my physical and emotional health. I followed Pesnyary on their tours, thoroughly enjoying myself, living in the shadow of Lenya's fame. This made it much easier for me to make a complete transition into a life without gymnastics. We started to work together on his career. I taught him how to move and how to look more relaxed onstage.

People who didn't know any better assumed that Lenya and I got married so that we could combine our 'fortunes'. Even the members of his group thought that he had married me for the money. But neither of us really had any. It's funny the musicians in the Soviet Union all thought the athletes were rich, and we thought the musicians were rich! My husband sold forty-five million records, and all that money went to the State. The only reward either of us ever got for our efforts was the sixteen dollars per diem, when we were travelling. That's *sixteen*, not sixty. No one could believe that we would go on tour in America, and earn so little. It was said that Pesynary got 30,000 dollars a week when they were in the United States, but the State (in this case, not the Sports Committee, but the Gros Concerts) took the profits for themselves. It was the usual thing: we did all of the work; they took all the money.

I was having a great time. I don't know what would have happened to me if I hadn't met Lenya. Thanks to him, I became a much nicer person. I'm sure he had a hard time with my explosive temperament, but I loved him very much, and we were both very happy.

There was one thing that made me wonder why he took the chance of marrying me. I had a physical flaw. After twelve years of abusing my body by not eating enough, and working much too hard, all the specialists told me that I would not be able to conceive a child.

When I broke up with the man I had been originally planning to marry, his response was, 'Who wants a sterile woman like you, except me?'

I worried lest that might be true, but Lenya and I were reconciled to the fact that we would never be blessed with children, and we delicately avoided the issue whenever possible.

However, a few months after we got married, I started having aches and pains. After all the injuries I had suffered doing gymnastics, I was accustomed to physical discomfort, so I didn't give it a second thought. I was as thin as ever, but I did feel a bit strange, as though something might be in there. So I went to the doctor, and he informed me that I was five months' pregnant.

We were very happy about this and before we knew it, four more months had passed. Actually, we completely lost track of the time. My hips were so narrow that the doctor had told me I would either need a Caesarean section or, if I wanted to have a natural childbirth, I should try to keep the baby very small. So I spent most of my pregnancy dieting. Until the very end, my stomach didn't show at all. I was still wearing my everyday jeans.

One day, I was cooking lunch when I felt a pain in my back. I figured that it was my old lumbago acting up. Then the pain became rhythmically worse, and I turned to Lenya.

'Something's wrong,' I said. 'Maybe I have a pinched nerve.'

So he called my mother who told us to go to the hospital immediately, right away, *right* now, because I was having contractions. But neither of us had realized that nine months had passed, so we didn't really grasp the urgency of the situation.

'You know what?' Lenya said when he had hung up the phone. 'Just wait a little bit, because I have a rehearsal. I'll go for a couple of hours, and we'll simply wait and see what happens.'

I said okay. But then, I couldn't stand it any more.

I called him up and said, 'I *really* can't hold it anymore, it hurts.'

'Okay,' he replied. 'Just wait a little while longer. I'll be back soon.'

When things became really unbearable, I called one of the other singers in the group and he arrived with an emergency ambulance. We were just leaving the house when Leonid showed up. I moved from the ambulance into his car to go to the hospital. He was so nervous that he could barely drive. At the hospital, he even lit up a pipe, although he had never smoked in his life.

A few hours later, Richard was born!

Chapter Sixteen

My son was born very small, but very healthy. In spite of my doctor's dire warnings, I didn't have a difficult labour at all. I think my gymnastics training really helped. My muscles were very strong, and I knew how to handle pain. This was in March 1979, and at time of writing, Ricky is about to turn thirteen.

We named him after Leonid's grandfather. Leonid comes from a very famous and aristocratic family in the Soviet Union, the Radzivils. During Stalin's repressions, his grandfather was sent to Siberia, because he was an ancestor of Polish-Lithuanian Prince Radzivillo and considered a possible trouble-maker. His life in Siberia was extremely difficult. Fortunately his eldest brother went there in 1946, and somehow got him out. He came home, saw everyone, and then he died. His last request was that at least one of his grandchildren should name his son Richard, and that the boy would then be very lucky.

We are the only members of Leonid's family who did this, and we think we are the lucky ones.

I spent most of the next five years completely devoting myself to my family. I cooked, cleaned the house, did the laundry and looked after Richard.

We were now living in Minsk, and when we had moved away from Grodno, I offered our apartment to my parents. Their reaction should not have surprised me, but it did.

Years earlier, after the Munich Olympics, Larissa Latynina had come to Grodno to visit me. When she saw our crowded room, her shock was visible, and she demanded to see a city official.

'How can you let our Olympic champion live like that?' she asked sanctimoniously. 'Where does she do her homework?'

It was one of the few nice things she ever did for me because, within days, the City Council came up with a two-bedroom apartment for my family.

My father was not happy about this. On the day we moved, he wandered from one corner to another on the old, squeaky floorboards. He stopped and fondly stroked the still-warm stove. All of a sudden, with an urgency that had been lacking for years, he started repairing a leaky tap. Then, while the truck driver in the yard honked his horn impatiently, my father opened the last box of our unpretentious belongings, took the record player out and put on a record we had always enjoyed listening to in the evenings. While the music played, he wept.

It is a sight I have never forgotten.

Leonid's and my apartment in the Regional Party Committee building was much nicer than my parents' place, and I thought they would be happier there. So I decided to talk to my father about the idea.

'Dad, why don't you take over my apartment?' I suggested one day. 'You and Mom will be comfortable here. I can arrange it for you.'

'No, Dochka,' he said, still using my childhood nickname after so many years. 'Your apartment is for big-shots. We are absolutely fine where we are. Don't worry about us.'

Although I knew that his humble pride would never have allowed him to accept my offer of help, I still felt very sad.

My life with Leonid and Richard (Rick for short) was hard, because we, too, were quite poor. Once, a week before payday, we even had to borrow a 'tenner' from our neighbours to get by. The only way we could survive was for my husband to keep going on tours with the band, and I would often accompany him. Usually, we would leave Rick with my mother, in Grodno. Before these trips, all my travels had been restricted to foreign cities. Atlanta, Singapore, London and New York were more familiar to me than the cities in my own country. Now I was seeing places such as Vladivostock, Irkutsk, Murmansk and Odessa, and I enjoyed the chance to get to know my homeland better.

Once, we were off with the band in the far east of the USSR when our room phone rang. When I answered, it was my sister Zina, sounding very cautious and tense.

'What is it?' I asked, already frightened.

'Come to Grodno right away,' she said. 'Something bad has happened.'

My parents. 'Father?' I guessed.

'Please come back,' she said. 'I'll tell you when you get here.'

I started my long journey from the extreme east of our vast country to the extreme west, trying to avoid panicking. My father. It had to be my father.

The trouble turned out to be even closer to home than that. Mother had been doing some laundry, and there was a tank of boiling water next to her. Little Rick had stumbled and fallen into that tank, receiving burns across twenty-five per cent of his body. By a stroke of luck, a bottle of sea buckthorn oil was near by, and my mother had reacted instantly, pouring the entire contents over his poor little body to minimize the damage.

While I had been en route to Grodno, the doctors had been trying desperately to save my child. Even after I arrived, it wasn't clear if he would survive. For three days, Rick was in shock, and very close to death.

I have never felt as hopeless and desolate as I did then.

He recovered, finally. The awful incident left tiny scars on his body and a huge welt on my soul. Oddly enough, he developed a unique immunity to fever as a result of his injury.

When we decided to have another baby, the pregnancy was neither secret nor unexpected. I seemed to have no trouble conceiving, now that my body was again functioning normally.

By the time the baby was due, my husband and I were wandering around our apartment like two shadows, waiting to go to the hospital. The phone rang constantly, as people all over the world were calling to see if I had yet gone into labour.

'Well?' they would say. 'Is it time to congratulate you yet?'

There were to be no congratulations at all. The doctors were negligent, and after being perfectly healthy twenty-four hours earlier, my baby was stillborn. We had even picked out a name for him – Ivanushka. I found out later from some specialists that if I had been put into hospital and kept under observation for a few days, the outcome would have been different.

In the following months, I felt very restless and unhappy. . . I needed to start doing something constructive with my life, but I couldn't seem to find an outlet for my energies.

Shortly after Rick was born, I had gone to the gym and started training strenuously. Why? I don't know. I even spread a rumour that I was going to attempt a comeback at the Moscow Olympics – and almost managed to make myself believe it.

After a month of training, I went to Grodno to show Ren how quickly I had restored all my skills and recovered from my pregnancy, and developed a powerful new arsenal of gymnastics exercises. I was missing only one ingredient: desire.

Ren gave me credit for my achievement, but remained silent beyond that. Both of us realized that it was impossible to bring back the past. Why did I even go to him? To show off, I guess. To remind him that he had never 'moulded a thousand girls like me'.

He never found another Korbut, and I never found another Knysh. But, for those few wonderful moments back in 1972, we had managed to capture lightning in our little bottle, and show it to the entire world.

For a long time I did my best to remain a part of the gymnastics world. I needed to fill my life with something, and gymnastics was what I knew. I decided to try to share my views about the sport and its prospects. I worked, in an advisory capacity, as a State Coach for the Belorussian branch of the USSR Sports Committee, so I set out to create favourable working conditions for talented coaches such as my sister Ludmilla. I spent time travelling around the Republic, arranging for accommodation and athletic training facilities for others. Amazingly, I ran into a lot of problems with our local authorities.

'Why are you making trouble, Korbut?' they would ask. 'Why are you sticking your neck out? Do you think you're the smartest person around?'

All I wanted to do was work, but no matter how hard I tried, people created problems for me. I was constantly writing applications and reports, dealing with mountains of junk, instead of accomplishing anything worthwhile.

In the end I decided to try some actual coaching. Ludmilla was going abroad to work for a while, and she had left her pupil, Galya Sushko, with Miligula, an army club coach.

'Let me try to work with the girl,' I suggested.

He was happy to be rid of her. 'For God's sake, take her!'

I coached Galya for only six months, and she won a silver medal at a national championship. Success! Now I could believe in myself again. But it didn't last long. A few days later, I called Galya to remind her about a work-out, and she sounded very strange.'

'I can't come, Olga Valentinovna,' she said. 'Miligula thinks I'd better not.'

Miligula resented and envied the success I had had with Galya, and decided to put an end to it. He had made no progress with her, yet could not accept that anyone else, especially me, could do better. She stayed with him and never won anything of note again.

Ren had run into the same problems, over and over, and in 1981, he lost his place permanently as a coach. The father of one of his students accused him of having sex with his daughter. The rumour spread all over the city, and an investigation was ordered. The suspicion turned out to be false. The girl was, in fact, a virgin. But Ren was never able to find another job in the sport again. Instead of giving up, he devised a modern gymnastics school project and offered it to various officials, but after some initial interest, his plan was treated with complete apathy.

Now I, too, was being pushed out of the sport. I kept trying to find a place for myself, but nobody seemed to want me. I even got the impression that some people in the system wanted every mention of me erased. There was no need to eliminate me physically; all they had to do was destroy the memory of my name.

As I already mentioned, they would never show tapes of me on Soviet television. Nowadays, when I watch gymnastics meets on television in Russia, I see elements I performed first which are identified with other people's names. A back lay-out dive through a chest roll, poorly done, is named after Lubov Bogdanova. Loops, now carelessly performed, all of a sudden are known as the 'Moukhina Loop'. Most young gymnasts in the Soviet Union today have never even heard the phrase 'Korbut Loop'. Some of them have a vague idea that I might have done it once, but that's all. Elements I performed for years were wiped out of the technical rules, or renamed. Perhaps they felt that if they ignored me, I might go away.

Looking back, maybe I could have continued my career, if I had gone about it in the traditional way. All I had to do was join the Communist Party, study at a Party school, and then I could have become the Belorussian Team Coach permanently. Without an official Party education, such a position is out of the question in our system.

I still have my application to the Party, although it seems silly when I read it now. At the time, I wrote what I thought I really felt:

I request admission to the Communist Party of the Soviet Union as a candidate member. Since the time I became aware of what life is, I have given all of it for the benefit of my great Motherland and our people. Like my parents, I have not renounced any of the glorious memories and I have tried not to live in vain.

I am driven by constant diligent labour and a feeling of pride for my people and the Party! Like every Soviet citizen and Young Communist League member, I want to join the

148

*ranks of the progressive Soviet youth. I will try to do every-
thing to enhance the glory of my people and to give my life,
the best I can, to the cause of Lenin and to the cause of
Communism.*

I was clearly naïve then, but I was sincere. I can thank Ren
for keeping all his gymnastics pupils in such a complete
vacuum. Not only was I unaware of anything else that was
going on in the world; I didn't even know that there *was*
anything else. When I retired and went out into the real
world, I was like an infant. I still resent the fact that he did
nothing to help me prepare for my future after gymnastics.
I think that this preparation is one of a coach's most important responsibilities and he failed miserably.

Many of us were dropped from the sport into a sea of
day-to-day problems. Tamara Lazakovich, Tonya Koshel,
Masha Filatova, Elena Moukhina, and dozens of other
talented gymnasts disappeared without a trace. Today, most
of them are living in extreme poverty.

I was bolder than many, and went to then Party Chief of
Belorussia, Pyotr Mironovich Masherov, when I retired.

'Pyotr Mironovich, I'm going to get married,' I told him. 'I
will need an apartment.' Luckily, he liked me.

I still hoped to be accepted by the sports leadership, but
in spite of my fervent letter, I was not admitted to the Party.
During the move from Grodno to Minsk, I lost my Young
Communist membership card, which was considered a very
serious crime. It showed that I could not keep documents
safely, and therefore could not be trusted. With that repri-
mand on my record, naturally I could not be allowed to join
the Party.

Nelli Kim, a former member of our National Team, moved
from faraway Chimkent to Minsk, and we became friends.
We would often talk together about our plans, and I told her
that it was my dream to coach the Belorussian team one day.
Despite this knowledge, Nelli entered a Party school and
was herself appointed Senior Coach of the Belorussian

National Team. I was hurt by this apparent betrayal, and resented that she was given the position since I knew her main interest was in travelling abroad. She was not at all concerned about the development of Belorussian gymnastics and the future of our local athletes.

I understand why they didn't give me the position. After all, I wasn't even a member of the Party. But why not give it to Voltchetskaya, or Alexayeva, my former coaches? These women knew and loved the republic, and its people – and they were excellent coaches. But nobody wanted to hear my objections and today, I think that gymnastics in Belorussia has died. It is very sad, and it didn't have to happen.

I was laid off, and my 'allowance for life' decreed by the Council of Ministers was rescinded. I was simply thrown away like a piece of junk. In despair, I decided to become a jockey, since I loved horses, and it was one of the few sports with no upper age limits. Every day, for several months, I took a train to the village of Ratomka, outside Minsk. There was a stable there and former Olympic champion Victor Ugryumov was the senior coach in charge of it.

I took care of the horses, feeding, washing and cleaning up after them. Being around those kind animals was so soothing that I finally felt cured of my restlessness. I went through a two-month training programme there, and did so well that Ugryumov was genuinely puzzled by my success.

It didn't hurt that I desperately wanted to return to big-time sports, but I think the fact that I really love animals also had a lot to do with it. I have spent my life surrounded by anything that can bark, meow, crawl or swim. In Grodno, we had rabbits, a pair of hedgehogs, a piglet and even a water snake.

Growing up, I also had a wonderful cat who was as black as tar. She was very clever and adroit, and a profoundly decent animal. She did not bring her numerous offspring to our small room, and I was very curious about where she might be hiding her kittens. Finally, I found them. All twelve were in the attic, starving.

I promptly went down to the kitchen and took every scrap of food I could find. The kittens finished the food in seconds, while their mother pretended not to be hungry at all. After that, the cats and I had a sort of conspiracy, and I would steal everything I could to feed them.

My parents finally caught me in the act of taking our much-needed food, but they liked cats almost as much as I did, so my punishment was not very severe. The kittens went to live with our neighbours, and were well fed from then on. But they never forgot me, and one or another of them often came over to 'say hello'.

We kept one of the male kittens for ourselves. He was the exact opposite of his mother – stupid and lazy – but we still loved him.

His mother was eight years older than *I* was, and I cried my heart out when she died. Shortly beforehand, she began meowing and scratching at the door. I fed her milk, and even found some fish for her, but she would just turn away, mourning miserably.

I did not understand that animals, like people, sometimes get old and die. My cat simply felt death coming, and wanted to be private. When I opened the door, she went out to our vegetable garden, where she died in peace. I buried my friend in the ravine in a grave with a small wooden cross on top of it.

Today, I still have animals in my home. Each time one of them dies, it is a tragedy for our family.

Anyway, my equestrian experiments ended abruptly. Ugryumov told me to ride quiet mares, since they are easier to control than stallions, but I thought I knew better. I mounted a young stallion, an as-yet-unbroken animal. I thought I could handle him, but he bolted, straight into the middle of the herd. Jealous mares indignantly nudged me off his back to the ground, and the last thing I remember is getting hit in the chest with a hoof.

I was haemorrhaging, and they barely managed to get me to the hospital in time. In the middle of the night, I started bleeding internally again. Several doctors consulted among themselves, and then went over to my worried husband.

'At any moment, there might be a third haemorrhage,' they told him. 'She won't survive it. We have to operate on her immediately.'

I was half out of it, but I managed to object.

'I won't survive an anaesthetic,' I mumbled. 'You can't operate.'

The doctors looked at one another.

'Okay, if that's what you want. . .' one of them said, and they returned to their warm beds.

Five minutes later, the third haemorrhage started. My husband started yelling and doctors from all over the clinic came running in. They decided that I needed a direct transfusion and one of the surgeons, Victor Roubashenko, volunteered.

My husband wasn't supposed to be in the operating room but he stayed. My doctor, Vyacheslav Kaplin, struggled to find a vein that hadn't collapsed so that he could use it for the transfusion. Roubashenko's blood saved my life.

Even now, nobody can explain how I managed to escape that close call. And I still love horses.

While I was in the hospital, I spent a lot of time thinking about what I was going to do with my life. I could not go on without a purpose or a direction.

I did not know that an event completely beyond my control was soon going to change the course of my life forever.

Chapter Seventeen

On 26 April 1986, a melt-down at the Chernobyl nuclear power plant exposed millions of Belorussians to radiation. We were living in Minsk, which is less than 200 miles away from the site, and well within the danger range.

For me, the story really begins with the fact that we were told nothing about the incident by the government. For days we had no idea that anything of this magnitude had occurred! We knew that there had been some kind of explosion, but it didn't sound all that serious, and the citizens of Belorussia were told nothing beyond that. So, not knowing about the radiation, we all kept drinking tap water, buying milk and eating fresh vegetables.

A week after the melt-down, we were told that we had to be evacuated because of the possibility of radiation poisoning. The officials told us that we risked thyroid damage and other unpleasant and dangerous side-effects. But by then, seven days after the explosion, it was too late. Everyone had already been exposed. The fall-out from the radiation would have been terrible enough, but our government's treachery made the situation even worse.

Some time later, my husband happened to be on a train and got talking with a Soviet nuclear scientist, who told him that the catastrophe at Chernobyl had been the result of an unfortunate military accident. The purpose of the plant had been to burn uranium, to manufacture plutonium. They were using the plutonium to make atomic bombs. If the power plant had only been working for peaceful purposes –

providing needed energy for the people of Belorussia – the by-products would *not* have been plutonium, and the accident would not have been as serious. Also, if it had been a normal power plant, the government probably wouldn't have tried to cover up the disaster.

My husband couldn't believe that the scientist was revealing to him all this shocking information, and exclaimed, 'What are you doing, talking to me? What if I worked for the KGB, and reported you?' The scientist was not alarmed at all. 'What's the big deal?' he responded. 'Everybody knows about this. Didn't you?'

No. We did not.

If our people had known that the power plant was working for defence purposes, they would have tried to close it down. That's why everyone accepted the information so readily when they heard about the 'accident'. As a result of our terrible system, no one ever knew what was really going on, and people got hurt. In this case, people died and are *still* dying.

My husband feels that maybe the accident was God's way of punishing the officials who were using the peaceful power plant for ugly military objectives; but unfortunately, millions of innocent people are also being punished. *Millions.*

They just didn't know.

As far as God is concerned, I'm not exactly sure what I believe, although Leonid is a Catholic. I became a Christian rather late in life, and by accident. I was in Moscow with Leonid's group, and we were having lunch in the Hotel Russia restaurant before his concert. Sitting nearby was a group of famous academics, who were celebrating somebody's Nobel Prize. They all recognized me, and when Leonid had to leave, they invited me to join them.

We sat and talked about life, and I told them that I really regretted never learning about religion. These men were very famous and honoured academics, and they were not afraid to talk about things like religion in public. They were amazed to hear that I had never been baptized, and they said, okay, tomorrow morning, at eight o'clock, there will be two black limousines waiting for you, and we will take you to the Nova Devichii Monastery. The Nova Devichii is the oldest and most famous monastery in Moscow.

I didn't believe them, since they had been drinking and celebrating at the time, but just in case, we waited out in front of the hotel at eight in the morning and, sure enough, there were two black Volgas waiting for us. We went out to the monastery, and I was finally baptized at the age of twenty-eight.

I had been wearing a cross for years, for symbolic reasons, but now it really *meant* something to me. I felt clean inside, and better as a person. I *do* believe that there is Someone out there – I don't know exactly who – but Someone who helps me to look at things differently. If something unpleasant happens, I try not to be hurt; I just say to myself, well, God must have wanted it this way. God predestined this, and now I have to work within the situation.

But Chernobyl is a hard one to understand because, more than anyone else, the radiation hurt our children. Every day, Belorussian children are dying. Most of them fall victim to leukaemia, but the radiation poisoning has also caused diabetes, bone diseases, blood and heart disorders, and brain cancers. And the smallest and weakest among us, the children, are the ones who are suffering the most.

I wanted to help, but I didn't know how. It was gymnastics that came to my rescue. Leonid and I had planned for years to revisit the United States, trying to go through official channels several times, yet were always refused. We were 'Nevyezdnoi' – unreliable, not subject to travel abroad.

Finally, a musician friend of Leonid's who was now living in the States sent us a private invitation, and we were able to go for a visit. After that, people seemed to remember me, and we were invited by the American Gymnastics Federation to go to Indianapolis, Indiana.

When people in Belorussia learned that we were going to the United States, many parents whose children had leukaemia and other terminal diseases caused by the Chernobyl disaster telephoned or came to see us to ask for help.

They brought blood samples and asked if there was any way we could get them analysed in America. There are really no comprehensive paediatric medical facilities in the republic of Belorussia. I particularly remember a cab driver named Sergei who sought me out just before we left.

'You are going to America,' he said. 'My daughter Irina Choukovski has leukaemia, and they cannot help her here. In the States, they have a clinic where they can save my daughter. Could you help us, please?'

I could certainly *try*. It took me *six months* to get permission from the State to take the several hundred glass slides of children's blood for analysis, but finally, our trip and my cargo were approved.

When we arrived in Indianapolis, my guide, turned out to be involved with the Red Cross, and she helped me get the blood samples to a local clinic for testing. The clinic agreed to help Irina, and as many other children as they could. In addition, the Red Cross started raising money for the innocent young victims of the Chernobyl nuclear catastrophe.

I also received a lot of attention from other sources in America. Nobody had heard anything about me for many years, and now that I had suddenly reappeared, many magazines and newspapers were interested in updating the Olga Korbut story.

'Where have you been for so long? Why didn't you come to receive the US Women's Foundation Prize?' people asked me. 'We sent you an invitation back in 1978.'

I blushed, and mumbled something incoherently. I was ashamed to tell them the truth: I did not get that invitation. It turned out that I had been sent invitations every year, showing that people in America still remembered and loved me. The Soviet leadership had decided not to bother sharing this information with me.

My trip to Indianapolis coincided with that of the USSR National Team, and I was asked to perform along with them. *Me?* Perform? After all these years? Before leaving Minsk, I went on a crash diet, and dropped from forty-five kilogrammes back to my Munich weight in a month. Restoring my gymnastic skills was a little more difficult. I don't think I got back to my prime form, but I did the best I could.

So many years had passed that when I first stepped out to the podium in front of an American audience, I wasn't sure what to expect. I stood in the spotlight and heard complete silence. Then the silence exploded into an ovation as heartfelt as the ones I had been given back in the early 1970s. My eyes filled with tears. I put a finger to my lips to still the crowd, and started my floor routine, accompanied by the familiar 'Kaleenka' tune. I was rewarded by thunderous applause.

I did eight performances in eight states, and received the same wonderful ovations each time. Thank you, America! Thank you for remembering me! I never forgot you, either.

I didn't know how much people knew about the situation in my country, so I decided to bring up Chernobyl at my first American press conference in Indianapolis, hoping to draw attention to the issue. I told the reporters about the many sick children, and about how our beautiful Belorussia had been utterly devastated by the effects of the radiation cloud. I showed the medical papers and blood tests I had been given by the desperate parents. I explained how terrible life had become for my people, and talked about the contaminated food, water and air. Everything was so bad in Belorussia. It was hard even for a *healthy* person to survive over there, let alone a sick child. I told the reporters all these things, and – I don't know why I was surprised – Americans opened their hearts to us.

First, a local hospital immediately contacted us, and invited us to tour their facilities. They showed us the modern techniques they used to treat leukaemia, and offered to do everything possible to help us. The Emergency Help for Children Foundation, Inc., a charity based in Carmel, Indiana, was formed to help the sick and dying children of Belorussia.

Unfortunately, nothing had changed back in the Soviet Union, and it took the authorities five months to prepare the documents to allow the taxi driver's sick daughter, Irina Choukovski, to come to the United States for treatment. By the time the papers were ready, the little girl had already died. Yet another tragedy that could have been prevented!

An American doctor, Dr Robert Gale, had come to the USSR shortly after the disaster to assess the damage. He predicted that there would be a terrible outbreak of leukaemia in my beloved Belorussia within three or four years. Our scientists, hoping to prevent a panic among the citizens, declared that this was impossible, and that the American doctor was simply incompetent.

But Dr Gale was right. Even as you are reading this, there are many children dying unnecessarily in the Minsk Haematological Centre. They are dying of leukaemia, because the Centre does not have the technology and medicines to help them. What could be more dreadful?

I had managed to get the blood samples to Indianapolis, but I wanted to do *more*. Instead of assisting me, my government did nothing but create interference. The APN News Agency, the Council of Ministers of Belorussia – no one I asked would help me. After many months, we managed to organize a centralized system to help transport the sick children to the United States, but I worried, based on previous experiences with Soviet officials, that the offspring of Party and Soviet leaders would be sent abroad instead of the children who were desperately ill.

Now, I had found my purpose. I had a goal far more important than anything else I had ever done in my life: to assist the children who have suffered the fate of experiencing, in peacetime, the likely consequences of a nuclear war. With the help of my many new friends in America, I began to devote my life to raising funds and helping those innocent children.

Leonid and I were worried that Richard's health might be affected by staying in Minsk, so during one of our trips to the States, we took the difficult decision to leave him behind with close friends in America. We hated to do it, but we didn't think we had any choice. Fortunately, we continued to receive invitations to visit the United States and continue our work. Finally, we were able to settle in New Jersey and be reunited with him.

My then manager was based in Seattle, Washington, and that is how we heard about the Fred Hutchinson Cancer Research Center. The Center is famous worldwide for its cancer research, particularly in the area of bone marrow transplants. We were very interested by this because, if chemotherapy doesn't work, a bone-marrow transplant is the only thing that will help cure a leukaemia patient. We went to the Center, and were amazed when they showed us the results of their efforts. Out of a thousand operations, almost eighty per cent had been successful! This is a phenomenal success rate.

I decided to set up the Olga Korbut Foundation, and use the money to work in conjunction with the Hutchinson Center. My hope was that by using my name, I would be able to increase our fund-raising abilities. Bone marrow transplants are very effective, but the treatment is extremely expensive.

I also want to build a hospital in Minsk because so many children die before they are able to get to America. Many people are supporting this idea, and the plan is to build a hospital similar to the Hutchinson Center. We hope that there will then be a sort of medical exchange programme. American doctors will go to Minsk to help diagnose and treat patients, and Belorussian doctors will visit America, study the most up-to-date techniques and return home to use their knowledge to help our people. Some of the money we are raising will help train these doctors, and another portion will be used to build the hospital.

So far, the foundation has managed to accomplish some wonderful things. Recently, we were able to help a young girl with five holes in her lungs. These holes may originally have been congenital defects, but they were so large that the unnatural growth could only have been the result of her exposure to radiation. She came to St Joseph's Hospital in Atlanta, Georgia. The hospital paid for her surgery. Her operation was on a Monday, and on Friday she went home from the hospital. It was wonderful. We are trying to make arrangements to keep her here in the States, so she can continue to receive the necessary medical attention she may require. Life is so hard in the Soviet Union these days, even for people who are not suffering from the lingering effects of the radiation. A loaf of bread used to cost 60 kopeks, and now it costs more than 12 roubles. This young girl's chances of making a full recovery are much better in the US, and we are working to do everything possible to assure her a safe and healthy future.

Now that I have settled in America, I am free to spend as much time as I want on foundation business, without running into any pointless interference from Soviet officials. Twice a year, I go back to Minsk on behalf of the foundation, but my life is in America now. I set up regular speaking engagements, and talk to interested groups to tell them about what is happening in Belorussia, and to explain how they can help. That, of course, means asking for donations. I don't really enjoy that aspect of my talks, but the Chernobyl disaster was several years ago, and people forget. In the meantime, children are dying every day. So little attention has been paid to them, and they need our help. My family, thank God, is healthy, but too many others are not as lucky.

Before I got so deeply involved in this issue, even I didn't realize how serious the situation was, and the degree to which the beautiful land of Belorussia was affected, and will continue to be affected, for decades. Radiation never disappears, and if people forget that, we have to keep reminding them.

I hope, and pray, that with continued research and treatment, we will be able to save every child who needs our help. I will continue to help them until the very last one is cured. It is the most important thing I have ever done in my life.

Chapter Eighteen

Today, my family and I are living outside Atlanta, Georgia, the site of the 1996 Summer Olympics. I spend a large portion of my time doing foundation business, but I have also started coaching at a local gymnastics centre. I guess no matter how hard I try, I can never *quite* get away from gymnastics. It seems to follow me wherever I go.

Today, I have the opportunity to develop *my* school of gymnastics, starting with the socks and ending with the smile! I have two main goals I want to accomplish in Atlanta.

First of all, I want to bring the best coaches here to work with our students. I have already invited the top coaches in the Soviet Union, and they have agreed to come. Once removed from the constraints and corruption of the Soviet sports system, they really are the best coaches in the world. Combining Russian and American coaching philosophies will be very successful.

American athletes seem to me very different from Russian athletes. Greatness cannot be achieved without taking risks, and Americans often appear afraid to do that. I am convinced that American gymnasts are very talented, but they don't seem to know how to *work*. Quite often, less talented athletes achieve more than the truly gifted ones because they work so much harder. You really have to be motivated, and American gymnasts seem to lack the enthusiasm and selflessness which are the keys to sporting achievement.

Gymnasts in this country take so much time off that it is

difficult for me to adjust to the schedule. They will take a three-day weekend, which is quite ridiculous. During those three days, a gymnast loses everything he or she has worked on during the week, and has to start all over again. In Russia, it is quite different. It depends, of course, on individuals, but when I was competing, I would never give myself a single day off. Even when my coach told me to take a Sunday break, I would still work. I wanted to keep my muscles in shape to prevent injuries. So I would run for at least an hour, and I would work with weights. They used to say that even if you woke me up in the middle of the night, I would still be ready to go out and perform, because I was in such great shape.

Another thing that is hard for many athletes to accept is that in big-time gymnastics, you cannot avoid occasional injuries. In fact, in the Soviet Union, we were taught that injuries help build your character. I know that sounds harsh, but how can you become a great athlete and not experience pain? Only I know how many broken bones and torn ligaments and joint dislocations resulted from the new elements Ren and I created. The Korbut Loop alone cost me three concussions. But there is no progress without risk.

Obviously, athletes should never ignore serious injuries like that, but they need to learn how to work through the minor ones, such as a blister on the hand. It will hurt for a little while and then it will go away. I spend a lot of time strengthening the kids' muscles so that they won't get hurt seriously. I try to prepare their bodies in every way possible. Sometimes injuries are unavoidable, but what many young gymnasts don't seem to realize is that when they are afraid to fall, they are more likely to do so. And if they are afraid, how will they ever be able to work on new elements? To compete at the international level, they need to move beyond those fears and self-inflicted limitations.

That is why, before I do anything else, I want to get the best coaches. Then, I want to create a school for coaches. A coach can hurt an athlete by being careless, but can equally do harm by being over-cautious. In America, coaches seem to support the athletes too much, supporting them too closely. Then the athletes will never be able to work *without* that help. My coaches never touched me, and I think that is part of the reason why I rarely felt fear. I always knew exactly what I could do, and exactly what it would feel like if I fell. And it wasn't so bad. I learned to just pick myself up and try again.

So I look forward to having coaches such as Ludmilla Zvonztova and Anatolyi Kazeev (both of whom worked with the USSR Olympic teams) come to Atlanta to help develop the American gymnasts of the future. Working together, we will all be able to learn so much from one another, and the athletes will benefit from this.

My main technique as a coach is to use a lot of feelings, teaching athletes to put part of themselves into their elements. Even when I performed the elements other people were also doing, I always performed them in a different way – *my* way. I would bring some little part of myself into the element, no matter how small it was, and then the element would be unusual in its own personal way. I want to help athletes find their individuality, and incorporate it into their routines.

There is no better coach than a person who has actually *done* everything they teach. That way, they not only instruct pupils in techniques but can also convey to students the feel of gymnastics when it is done properly.

Imagine that I am performing an element on the beam – a flip. Just before I do it, I think, *legs.* That's my technique. My body is one line, and I see that one line, and then it will work. So if the coach has never done these things, and just tells the student that he or she has to do it a certain way, it's not the same. But I can explain how it really *feels*, and I want to work with other coaches who look at gymnastics the same way. Without that kind of vision, we won't accomplish anything.

The important thing, therefore, is to find good coaches, and teach them these techniques. They can then train other coaches, who will go on to teach our next generation of athletes. The coaches will all be completely prepared, and will share their ideas and philosophies with their students. That way, we will all be working in the same direction. And this is the ideal way to coach athletes for the Olympic team.

My other goal in Atlanta is to create a residential gymnastics academy, similar to the tennis academies that have developed players such as Monica Seles and Jennifer Capriati. I would like to have a school where children who *want* to be gymnasts more than anything else can come to learn the sport. It would teach traditional subjects, along with intensive gymnastics practice and training. Three hours of school, then three hours of gymnastics, and so on. They would have time to study, time to train, time to play – and time to make friends. Ideally, the school could accommodate 300 to 400 specially selected students. Out of that number, surely a few great ones would emerge.

We will choose these athletes from all over the country. Children who are seriously interested would be invited for an audition. We will also travel around the country setting up clinics, where more athletes will be selected. Then, with some time at the International Gymnastics Clinic which is held in Pennsylvania each year, even more athletes will be discovered. The best athletes from all over the country will go there.

Talent is important, but I will also look for motivation. Attention will be paid to how quickly they seem to comprehend instructions, and how well they listen. We will also look at their flexibility and strength. We definitely will *not* overlook a 'fatty'. The school will take ten- and eleven-year-olds, and a few twelve- and thirteen-year-olds. The athletes must be old enough to know what they want, but young enough to be moulded into Olympic athletes. It takes *years* to train an Olympic athlete, and ten or eleven years old is a good time to start.

Eventually, we hope an Atlanta gym will become international. The great thing about America is that there are so many different nationalities here. I maintain that all people are equal, that we're brothers and sisters. It's time to throw out all this nonsense about 'national differences'. I don't care who I work with, whether they are Americans, Soviets or Japanese, black or white or brown. The most important thing is for them to work to develop their talents, and to be happy.

I think it is unforgivable to have so much experience, and not pass it on. I love it when my students perform an element they have never done before, and their eyes open wide with excitement. I want them to learn everything I can teach them so that they, in turn can develop the sport further, and continue the job I started. I hope that with the help of a good team of people, I can bring my ideas to life. This makes me feel that I have been born again, and that anything is possible.

Right now, I'm afraid that the future of gymnastics is very uncertain. I don't see any 'stars' in gymnastics today. The sport needs at least one bright star who can lead the way, and I don't see anyone who can do that.

The main goal in gymnastics, as I have said repeatedly, is to amaze the audience. For too long, the sport has been rooted in one place, and it needs to move forward. After my fall in Munich, when I got so much sympathy, it almost became the fashion for girls to burst into tears every time they fell. Yet spectators remained unmoved. Cheap tears are no way to buy people's emotions. The audience knows what is genuine, and what is not.

In due course, even these crocodile tears disappeared from gymnastics, along with most other visible emotions. Today, little girls seem to approach the apparatus like robots. There are no smiles, no happy expressions. With stone faces, they set about their hard, joyless work. Their routines are crammed with super-difficult elements. The audiences have become bored. Attendance at competitions has dropped all over the world. Today's gymnastics has become very complicated, and very dull.

I always wanted to do something new and exciting that

would be a revelation for the audience. I think that is why they applauded me. The audience needs to feel a connection with the athlete, and a personal stake in what she is doing. Otherwise, why watch at all? Today's gymnastics are just too impersonal, and all the 'tricks' in the world won't change that. Besides, revelations performed twice, let alone three or more times, are no longer revelations.

I have an idea that might help re-energize the sport. What if there were two categories? One could be for girls not older than sixteen or eighteen, and the other for older gymnasts who, though no longer able to do the more difficult elements, would be enriched by their experience, and could present more mature, fully realized routines.

During the last few years of my career, when my body could no longer take the stress of certain elements, I started to perform more as a dancer and actress, and the audience seemed to love it. I had so much confidence in my abilities that I could explore all possibilities.

I would appear suddenly unexpectedly at exhibitions to surprise the audience. Every night, I tried to do something new. I would go to the pianist and say, 'I'll do Kaleenka now', and he would reply, 'But we haven't practised.' 'That's okay,' I would answer, 'just play an introduction, and then I'll do it.' Once, before a performance – I think it was in New York – someone gave me a beautiful rose. I took the flower, and put it behind my back. The music was already playing, and I walked out and started to play with the rose. It became part of my performance, and then I gave it to the crowd when I was finished. Improvisations were fun for me, and fun for the audience.

At present a gymnast's career is over at eighteen or nineteen. If there were two categories, her working life would be much longer. There would be different rules for each, and different competitions. And, I can assure you, more people would watch the older group because their performances would be more interesting. Given the mature feminine figures, the lines of their bodies would be more beautiful.

If you think about it, I could perform even now! I couldn't compete with the younger gymnasts, but within my age category, I could do tremendous things. I really think that this is the future of gymnastics.

We would have to work it all out with the International Gymnastics Federation, but the older group should be professional, and get paid for their performances. That way, instead of having to retire, gymnasts would be able to support themselves. It would give them a much longer life in the sport. So many athletes leave, and end up in terrible situations because they don't have any money, or any skills beyond gymnastics. I can hardly think of a single major Soviet sports star who enjoyed a good life after his or her career was finished. If people in the United States and Europe hadn't known about me, and remembered me, I think I would have just disappeared, too. But if athletes were able to continue making a good living, there would be many more happy endings.

This is an innovative idea, and probably the athletes themselves would need some convincing. But I think it would really work. It would bring back our audiences, and that would help the sport as a whole. Everything we do, we do for people to enjoy, and I think the International Gymnastics Federation often forgets this.

Americans need to be more involved in the sport. This year, an American girl won the World Championship, and that's good. The more success the United States has, the more influence it will have with the International Federation. At this point, Americans barely participate in the International Federation, so they aren't aware of all of the intrigues and politics that poison the sport. As American gymnasts improve, they will start to fight for their existence, and the sport will change for the better.

What I really want is for gymnastics to be *fair*. The kids work so hard, and I don't want them to turn away from the sport. Too many of them already do, and without them, there *is* no sport.

People always ask me, how do we find another Olga

Korbut, and I say, maybe she hasn't yet been born. Or maybe we just haven't looked hard enough.

There have been plenty of Olympic champions over the years, and sometimes I wonder why I am among those whom people still remember. I think that if I *hadn't* fallen from the bars that awful night in Munich, I would have occupied a completely different place in history. But my uncontrollable tears really made the audience there in the arena – and television viewers all over the world – feel for that young gymnast from distant Belorussia. The little girl with the funny pigtails, who only the day before had amazed them with her perfect execution of incredible stunts, fell from her pedestal almost as quickly – and then climbed right back up again. No one could remain impassive looking at a little girl whose hopes had been broken against the foam rubber matting of Munich. Those seconds of stunned silence, followed by the ovation, and those thousands of telegrams and bouquets of flowers showed me how much all those people cared. They were with me, and they were *for* me. And I felt the same love for them.

Who knows how my life would have turned out if I had not fallen that night? I think that fall may have been the best thing that ever happened to me.

Today, I am at peace. I have finally found my place, with my work for the foundation and my coaching. My life has had its ups and downs, but at least it has always been *interesting*. I am happy to be here in America, and look forward to whatever comes next in my life.

The best thing about the unknown future is that it always looks so very bright.

The children of Belorussia continue to suffer, and much more work still needs to be done. We would be grateful for any help that people would like to give us.

Donations may be sent to:

The Olga Korbut Foundation
The Fred Hutchinson Cancer Research Center
1124 Columbia Street
Seattle, WA 98104
USA
(206) 667–2856